# THE
# ENGLISH
# COUNTRY
# CHURCH

# THE
# ENGLISH
# COUNTRY
# CHURCH

## Donald Sinden

With Illustrations by A.E. Fuller

SIDGWICK & JACKSON

LONDON

First published in Great Britain in 1988
by Sidgwick & Jackson Limited
1 Tavistock Chambers, Bloomsbury Way
London WC1A 2SG

ISBN 0 283 99504 1

Designed and produced by
Bellew Publishing Company Limited
7 Southampton Place, London WC1A 2DR

Printed and bound in Holland by Roto Smeets Ltd

Frontispiece:
*front cover of A. E. Fuller's
sketchbook folder,
showing the Parish Church
at Horsham, West Sussex.*

*To the memory of*
*my grandfather*
*Albert E. Fuller*

*Corner turret housing the spiral staircase*
*at Hoo in Kent.*

# Contents

# Acknowledgements

I am indebted to Joy Sinden, Leon Sinden,
Jeremy Sinden, Marc Sinden, and especially Roger
Godfrey, for allowing me to reproduce drawings
from their collections.

EXETER CATHEDRAL

*The magnificent western towers of*
*Exeter Cathedral, Devon.*

*Albert Emanuel Fuller.*

# Preface

*'Look up! Look up! You will see very little of*
*interest down there, but look up there . . .'*

This advice of my grandfather led me to a new field of observation – the light catching the foliage of trees, the higgledy-piggledy pattern of roofs, clouds scudding across the sky. He would say, 'Look at those street lamps – that one was made at the time of George IV, the other is late Victorian, can you see the difference? . . . Look at those chimney stacks – no two the same – you could make a study of those alone. Now here is All Saints – has your mother taken you in here? She hasn't? Oh good. The main part of a church is called the "nave" because it is like a big ship, and *navis* is the Latin word for ship, which is why we call our ships the Navy. Are you doing Latin at school? You're not? What a pity. The part over there, up that step, leading to the big window, is the chancel. That window is always in the east. Remember I showed you my compass? The porch we came through is in the south. You will always find the oldest graves on that side of a church because people were superstitious about being buried on the north side – the dark side. Nearly all old churches have been altered and have had pieces built on a long time ago. That window was put in when I was the same age as you are now – when Queen Victoria was on the throne.

'We had better be on our way home . . . That house over there is built of flint, the hard stones that are found in the chalk Downs or on the beach. The fishermen's houses in old Brighton – it was called Brighthelmstone then – were built of those. Better houses used flints that had been "knapped", or chipped carefully with another stone or a hammer until the surface was flat. Richer people had the flints knapped into square shapes so that they could be used like bricks, using less mortar than this house – some fine examples can be seen all over Sussex for grand buildings such as Goodwood House, St Pancras church in Chichester, or St Michael's in Lewes.

'Next week I will take you to see an old man who still knaps flintstones. You have probably heard at school that Stone Age man used flints as arrowheads . . . I wonder what Mummy has got us for tea?'

My grandfather, Albert Emanuel Fuller, died when I was quite young, but I still remember him vividly. Half an hour spent in his company was a voyage of discovery: I always came away with my imagination stimulated.

He was born in Brighton in 1865 of humble parents. He should have become an artist, but several things mitigated against this. Owing to the early death of his father, his widowed mother had to make provision for her family – six sons and a daughter – and this she did with great determination and enterprise, and encouraged the highest endeavour from her family. The boys were expected to earn their livings as soon as possible.

Albert was then 12 years old, his feet planted very firmly in the Sussex soil. He was observant of everything around him and, from an early age, had shown an aptitude for drawing, so he went through the conventional training then offered by art schools, while in his spare time he faithfully recorded the buildings and details which interested him. Unfortunately, colour-blindness prevented his development, but he was undoubtedly talented and his lifetime of sketching buildings has left us with what is now a valuable record.

The Lord's Prayer & The Belief
Written on the size of a threepenny piece
by A.E. FULLER

He was given a job in the Borough Surveyor's Department at Brighton and, in 1890, married Hannah Mary Corney – as I remember her, a very erect formidable figure with her hair pulled back and wearing pince-nez. My mother Mabel was born in 1891, followed by three more daughters: Edith (1894), Winifred (1897) and Florence (1900). With a family of his own now to support, my grandfather was delighted to be offered the position of Assistant Borough Surveyor to the contiguous town of Hove – a position he held until his regrettably early death.

However, this secure employment did not satisfy his inquisitive brain. The memories of my mother and aunts recalled a household which revolved around his fertile interests in which they too became involved. They learned to use his new microscope for which he made slides of insects and cross-sections of anything he could lay his hands on.

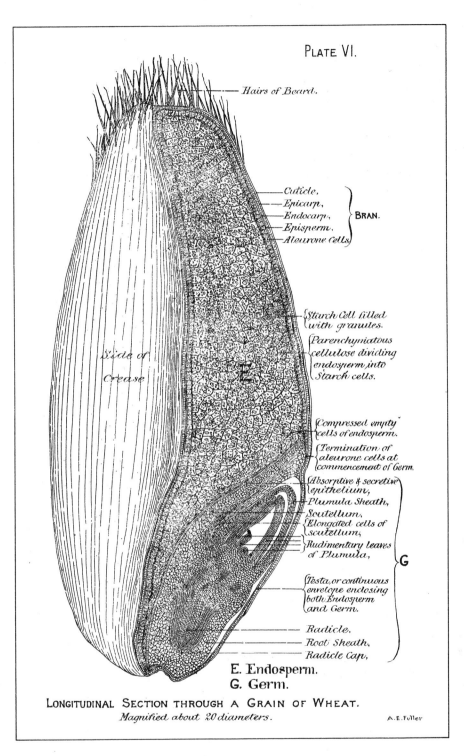

PLATE VI.

Hairs of Beard.

Cuticle,
Epicarp,
Endocarp,
Episperm,
Aleurone Cells

} BRAN.

Starch Cell filled
with granules.

Parenchymatous
cellulose dividing
endosperm into
Starch cells.

Compressed empty
cells of endosperm.

Termination of
aleurone cells at
commencement of Germ.

Absorptive & secretive
epithelium,
Plumula Sheath,
Scutellum,
Elongated cells of
scutellum,
Rudimentary leaves
of Plumula,

G

Testa, or continuous
envelope enclosing
both Endosperm
and Germ.

Radicle.
Root Sheath,
Radicle Cap,

Side of
Crease

E

E. Endosperm.
G. Germ.

LONGITUDINAL SECTION THROUGH A GRAIN OF WHEAT.
Magnified about 20 diameters.

A.E.Fuller

A detailed section of a grain of wheat.

*Village houses clustered round the church at*
*West Chiltington, West Sussex.*

He recorded their voices on the cylinders of his home-made phonograph. He built himself a special camera and took photographs of his family which, after he did his own developing and printing, could be viewed apparently in three dimensions through his own handmade stereoscope. He made several pieces of furniture from old and redundant church pews picked up on his travels. He experimented with the use of plaster of Paris by taking casts of the hands of his children and modelling portraits of his family on plaques. Prowling around one day in the vaults below Brighton Pavilion, he found the dismembered pieces of an enormous chandelier that had once hung in the Royal stables (now Brighton's concert hall, The Dome) and, in his spare time, re-assembled it so that it could be restored to its original position. He acquired many beautiful instruments, such as a machine for recording wind pressure (called, I understand, an anemometer), as well as his personal collection of surveying instruments, all made of brass and steel: his rules were of ivory, and all these things were housed in polished mahogany boxes and, to this day, are an endless source of interest and entertainment.

Wherever he went, he carried with him a sketchbook and numerous pencils – from 6B to 6H – to record the architectural delights that met his eye. His idea of a perfect holiday was to take his family and their bicycles on a train to a given

GODALMING
1911.

My aunts Winifred and Florence at play, while my
mother assists her father with his drawings.

*Riverside view of the village and its church tower*
*at Arlington, Kent.*

destination and to spend two weeks sketching all that interested him within the radius of a day's ride. Most of his drawings are still extant and most are dated, so I have recently been able to pinpoint the places where they must have stayed in different years. My mother often told me of these holidays and of their continued fascination: of how every outing was made exciting by new observations as they pedalled along; of how she would sit beside her father while the younger children played and pass him the required pencils as she watched the drawings take shape beneath his busy fingers; of how she listened intentively as he described the finer points of architectural details – the label stops, the mouldings, the corbels, crockets, cusps and quoins, the bosses, the voussoirs and blind arcades . . .

Many decades later, his last remaining daughter, my Aunt Florence, said, '— but your mother was the only one of us who really enjoyed those holidays – the rest of us were thoroughly bored sitting around waiting for him to finish yet another sketch.'

After my grandfather's death, my mother continued my architectural education and imbued me with the same fascination for observation. With her, I developed my interest in ecclesiology – the name by which the study of church architecture is known. Numerous learned books have been written on the subject in general and on various particular aspects such as stained glass, fonts and misericords – there is even a splendid new one on kneelers (hassocks) – so at the end of this book, I will give a list of books for further reading that may interest you. Meanwhile, with the help of my grandfather's drawings, I will attempt to lure you along the trail that has absorbed me.

Racing along the monotony of a motorway or railway, we see the landscape of England punctuated by the spires and towers of our parish churches, and our eyes are immediately attracted to them: 'Oh look! Quick, look – over there – isn't that lovely – a perfect English village with its church in the middle – where is it? Oh dear, if only we had time . . .' Or how often have we followed

*The village church and ancient farm buildings beside the village pond at Ditchling, East Sussex.*

17

*A church stands isolated, possibly the village houses
have moved elsewhere.*

*A quiet leafy lane, perfect for a bicycle ride.*

directions and arrived by car at the strange town or village of our destination and had to enquire for the centre? The answer is always: 'Near the church', the spire or tower of which can be seen from streets away. What a pity we don't have time to go in . . .

Next time, make time.

The best means of transport of all is the bicycle – up and over the next hill, down this lane, and there before us lies a quintessential English rural scene. Beside a village pond, a group of ancient farm buildings lean against a churchyard wall, and above them rises the stumpy spire and lichen-covered roof of the village church. Or the church may stand beside a manor house on the outskirts of the village, perhaps with a vast dovecote (delightfully pronounced 'doocut') nearby. Inside are thousands of little nesting boxes, and the doves and pigeons who used them provided the owner with eggs and very tasty pigeon pies. Or we may even find the church now isolated in a field because the village has inexplicably moved to another site. Or we may find all the village houses tightly clustered around the church as if huddling together for warmth. With luck, we may have already heard, across the meadows, the bellringers practising their changes. Close by is bound to be the oldest inn in

*An easy walk from the Great House to the church,*
*West Hoathly, West Sussex.*

*A vast dovecote, probably in Kent. I wonder if it*
*still exists?*

*A magnificent timbered inn, Bishop's Stortford,
Hertfordshire.*

the village (possibly appropriately named The Cross Keys, The Angel, The Bell or The Lamb).

Which shall we visit first? The average visitor will know more about the contents of the pub than the contents of the church, but with a little application, this can soon be rectified and – as with everything – the more you know, the more exciting your experience will be. But be warned, this hobby – let us call it by its proper name, ecclesiology – can become an obsession. There are over 16,000 parish churches in England alone, and every one of them is worth some hours of your time. And please remember to contribute as much as you can afford towards the upkeep of each church. They are our heritage and if we who love them don't give, who will?

So come with me.

## Part One

# A History of English Church Architecture

# The
## Saxon Churches

In the earliest English houses, the fire was kindled in the middle of the floor and the inhabitants arranged themselves in a circle around the blazing wood while the acrid smoke escaped through a hole in the roof. Then someone had the clever idea of directing the smoke up a stone- or brick-built chimney; however, such a chimney could be more solidly constructed if incorporated into the fabric of the house so that it became part of a wall. The inhabitants then arranged their chairs in a semi-circle around the fire, and this remained the seating plan in most houses for nearly a thousand years until, in the 20th century, central heating became the vogue. Since open fires were no longer necessary, fireplaces and chimneys were also redundant. For some decades, living-rooms lacked a focus, but now in many sitting-rooms – dare I say, most – the furniture is arranged around the flickering screen of a television set.

Likewise, so much of our church architecture has evolved over the centuries. This evolution was governed by ecclesiastical ritual, and because of this, it is necessary for me to start at the beginning.

Christianity was first brought to England in the mid-6th century by missionary monks from Ireland who, after their voyage across the Irish Sea, travelled either on foot or by horse and cart. Certainly by the time that St Augustine (who had been sent from Rome by Pope Gregory in 597) arrived in England, he found that Bertha, the wife of Ethelbert, the King of Kent, was not only a Christian, but had her own church in Canterbury. St Augustine therefore decreed that Canterbury should be the Christian 'headquarters'.

In each village that those first Celtic monks visited, they would find a convenient hillock on which to stand as they preached the Word, baptised the converted and elevated the Host to celebrate Communion. The monks marked these meeting places by erecting wooden crosses which, in villages with a strong Christian commitment, were replaced in time with crosses of stone, often beautifully carved with Celtic ornamentation, many of which can still be seen today. Quite often, these early meetings took place within the stone circles left over from the old pagan religions. These were accepted gathering sites, and the monks could triumphantly exorcise the ghosts of the primitive

cults. Many of today's churchyards follow the same circular plan of pagan stone circles – indeed, many of the old pagan customs and symbols were freely adapted to conform to the new religion. For example, the fact that the Sabbath is on a Sunday recalls the time of the sun worshippers, and several so-called 'Christian' saints were originally minor pagan gods. In many churches, we can find images (either carved or painted) of the 'Green Man' – a human face peering through a mask of foliage – who was a primitive spirit of the forest and provider of a plentiful harvest. Likewise, we can find images of the earth goddess known in Gaelic as *Sheela-na-gig*, which in turn is the origin of the Australian term 'a sheila'.

England's weather has always been notoriously unpredictable, and many a monk was soaked to the skin before they took to erecting a sort of sentry box, a semi-permanent shelter large enough for themselves and the Sacrament placed on a small portable altar. (The following three illustrations I drew myself!)

Eventually, monks began to visit villages quite regularly, especially those where they had left converted communities, so it seemed a sensible idea to install there permanent 'sentry boxes'. It didn't take long for the villagers to realize that, while the monks and the Sacrament were protected from the weather, they themselves were still getting wet, so they built special sheds large enough to cover the congregation and open at the end facing the monks' 'sentry boxes'.

This arrangement was still quite draughty until some local Pythagoras worked out the brilliant plan of joining the two structures together. Thus was the first church building created. Some pedants will disagree, but I stick to my theory.

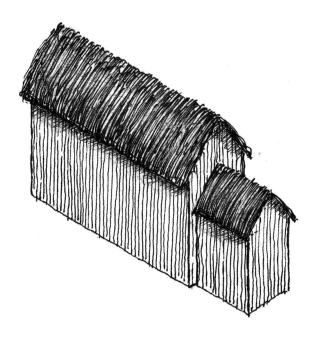

You can get some idea of what the early wooden churches looked like if you make a pilgrimage to Greensted-Juxta-Ongar in Essex, where the ancient oak-built nave of St Andrew's church, built more than 1000 years ago, can still be seen.

The land on which these new churches were built was inevitably owned by the local chieftain, or *thegn*, and building permission would not be given if the thegn were not himself a Christian. He would also want to keep an eye on the place, especially as he would be expected to pay quite a large proportion of the cost. As a result, in part for the sake of convenience, the church was either built in the grounds of his own estate or he built a new house next to the church, which accounts for the proximity of these two main structures in so many villages to this day. The original parishes also followed the boundaries of the thegn's domain, and annual 'beating of the boundaries' made sure that the thegns of adjoining villages had not encroached on his land in the previous twelve months. In addition, although the parish priest was subject to the authority of the Pope in Rome, the thegn could not allow his own temporal authority to be undermined, so he reserved the right to choose his own priest, to have the 'gift of the living' – a right still enjoyed by many present-day Lords of the Manor.

Time went by, congregations grew, and for regular use a bigger building was needed made of a more durable material than wood, such as stone – but stone was expensive. Fortunately, there were 'supplies' of ready-dressed stone available in many parts of the country: when they retired from England, the Romans left behind thousands of superb stone or brick houses and forts which had then fallen into ruination, and these were happily plundered by the early Saxons. For instance, many churches in Northumberland owe their stonework to Hadrian's Wall.

So now we see the typical Saxon church – still with the smaller section for the priest and the larger for the people. These became, respectively, the chancel and the nave. I mentioned earlier that England was host to missionaries from Ireland in the north-west and to missionaries from Rome in the south-east, and this somewhat confusing dichotomy produced some strange effects. Those from Rome built their chancels with a semi-circular or polygonal *apse* at the eastern end, while those from Ireland kept their chancels square at that end. For some reason, the English preferred the Celtic idea, and consequently, many apsidal chancels were reconstructed, and from then on, practically every English church had a squared chancel. Conversely, the English preferred the Roman liturgy, and this was soon in use throughout the country, which must be why they became known as 'Roman' Catholics rather than 'Irish' Catholics.

Because the priest was the only person allowed in the chancel where he said the Latin Mass, this part of the church soon assumed an air of mystery – a mystery fostered by the priest as he was the only man with the answers. Not until the Reformation, and the translation of the Bible into English so that it could be read by laymen, were all parts of a church incorporated in one room

*A semi-circular apse. Note the corbels under the*
*tower roof line, Newhaven, East Sussex.*

*The old stone bridge at Bradford on Avon, Wiltshire.*

under one roof. The perfect little Saxon church of St Laurence at Bradford on Avon in Wiltshire is high on the list of any aspiring ecclesiologist, but inexplicably my grandfather failed to record it at the same time as he did the above drawing of the beautiful bridge there.

However, here is a ground plan of St Laurence, without its porch – the better to illustrate my theory.

It is quite amazing that it was 'lost' for centuries until the local vicar, in 1856, cleverly spotted the tell-tale roof line while studying an old print of the town. Apparently the Normans built a much larger church further down the hill to accommodate the town's growing population, leaving the Saxon one forlorn and empty and to be used for nefarious purposes until its discovery in Victorian times.

My grandfather's drawing opposite is of the Saxon tower of the Parish Church of St Mary at Sompting in West Sussex. Nobody seems to know why it was given the unique helmet-like tower.

*The 11th-century tower of the Parish Church of*
*St Mary, Sompting, West Sussex.*

From the earliest days, it became the practice to place the altar at the east end of a church so that the congregation faced it from the west. There are several theories as to why this should be, but the one I like best is this: When the first Christian churches were built in the lands around the Mediterranean Sea, those erecting them tried to place the altars on the exact spots where martyrs had been executed or buried, and following pagan custom, the rest of the buildings, where the worshippers would be, stretched out to the north – i.e. the altar would be at the southern end. This held good until a church was proposed for the spot where St Paul was beheaded beside a main road in Rome. However, if the altar were placed on that spot, the rest of the church, if it had been built to the north, would have completely blocked the road. So they turned the altar and the church sideways, and from that time, all Christian churches followed the same plan – the altar in the east, the congregation in the west. Can you think of a better explanation?

If you were to try building a rectangular room with bricks, you would soon find that the walls need to be 'tied' together at the corners. Stone was the most durable material, but was not always accessible; it had first to be quarried and then transported and was therefore expensive. As a result, the larger blocks were usually reserved for the corners, and the rest of the walls were only faced with stone, and filled with rubble. A Saxon corner was made like this:

*'Long-and-short work' in the corners of the
tower walls at Sullington, West Sussex.*

For fairly logical reasons, this is known as 'long-and-short work', though I've never been quite sure which is the long and which the short! I should tell you that one of the best examples of this can be seen on the tower of All Saints church in Earls Barton in Northamptonshire.
(Be warned, you will soon find yourself travelling halfway across the country just to look at a window or doorway!) The interior of the church was lit by very small windows, deeply splayed to allow maximum light through the smallest aperture. The top of each window was made either triangular like this (Another of my illustrations. I wish my drawing was as good as my grandfather's.)

33

or was made of two small arches, sometimes carved from only one stone, divided with a stone pillar, like these

*Saxon openings at St Michael's church, Oxford.*

It was not long before the builders became more adventurous and began to incorporate towers into their churches. These were usually placed at the west end, but occasionally they were in the middle, between the nave and the chancel. These towers served many purposes. The top was useful as a look-out platform in times of war, and frequently large iron braziers were erected on them – a bonfire lit in one of these would be seen in the next village so that a message could be fired across England within minutes. Certainly these were used as the Spanish Armada approached our shores, and gave Sir Francis Drake ample time to make his final arrangements.

*View showing the window in the gable of the nave
at Singleton, West Sussex.*

Immediately below the top of the tower were hung the bells; louvred openings in the walls allowed the sound to travel. The floor below provided accommodation for the priest (fireplaces and chimneys can sometimes be seen), and windows were cut through into the nave so that he could see the altar and thus recite his office in the middle of the night without having to get out of bed. Sometimes rooms were constructed in the roof of the nave, with an entrance from the tower and a window at the other end, over the chancel. The best example of this is at Singleton in West Sussex, where this stained glass window was the only one in the church not smashed by Parliamentary troops during the Civil War, obviously because they failed to detect the room in the roof.

Towers are also assumed to have been used for defensive purposes and for the storage of weapons belonging to the villagers.

Now we come to arches . . . There is no other way – I will have to take you back to the ancient Greeks. I will be as quick as I can and it should be fairly painless.

When these amazingly civilized people first began to build temples, they made them from wood on a good flat foundation: several upright tree trunks, a big beam across the top and a sloping thatched roof. The result looked a bit like a Swiss chalet.

Then, about 2500 years ago, they abandoned wood and used instead the plentiful local marble. However, they retained the same basic design, even trying to make the marble look like wood. The columns are the tree trunks, the entablature (the part above the columns and below the roof) is the main beam,

and the triglyphs (the fluted blocks under the roof) appear to be the ends of other cross beams.

They never thought of using an arch.

You need an arch when you cannot find a single piece of stone long enough to span two uprights. The Greeks seem to have had enough long pieces of stone to suit their purposes so they just never needed an arch. Builders had to wait several centuries before a Roman discovered that if he made a semi-circular frame of wood between two stone uprights and then placed a series of stone blocks around it, their own weight would prevent the stones from collapsing when he took away the wooden frame.

He had invented the arch.

This same semi-circular arch was used throughout the Roman Empire. Even though the Empire itself collapsed and Roman buildings crumbled into ruins, these arches remained standing in theatres, baths and aqueducts, and were copied by later generations. In Britain, the Saxons used the Roman arch

*The Roman arch used in a primitive form at
Worth, West Sussex.*

in a primitive form, but it was not until the Normans arrived in 1066, bringing with them superior skills and techniques, that the arch was used to full effect. Typically, we British called it the Norman arch, while the rest of Europe continued to give credit to the Romans: they call it Romanesque.

*Splendid Norman arch with lectern,*
*Burpham, Sussex.*

St. Germans.
Cornwall.

*Highly decorated Norman doorway with row upon row
of carved mouldings.*

# The
# Norman Churches

A riot of church building followed the arrival of the Normans, but they took very few risks. Their walls were massive – sometimes four feet thick – while the windows, though bigger than the Saxons, remained very small. Now, however, the doorways assumed much greater importance and were decorated with row upon row of carved mouldings, each with a different name.

If you place a round-headed arch around a square-headed door, you are left with a semi-circular space above the door. This area is known as the *tympanum*, and the Normans filled it with splendid carvings befitting the entrance to God's house.

As the population increased, ever larger churches were needed. New ones were frequently built in the shape of a cross, giving north and south *transepts* – as the two wings are called – with, more often than not, a central tower as at Shoreham-by-Sea in West Sussex.

*One of Shoreham's two splendid churches.*

If it were a question of enlarging an existing church, the simplest way was to erect another building parallel to the nave and knock down the wall in between. However, even the stupidest builder knew that if he knocked down the whole wall the roof would fall in, so it needed to be supported by columns at regular intervals, with arches connecting them. This formed an arcade, with massive Norman columns supporting massive Norman arches supporting massive Norman walls. When this was done, the wall above the arcade remained intact and is quite often where the earliest construction can be seen.

Each arch or section is called a *bay*. The supporting columns, or piers, comprise three elements: the *base*, the *shaft* and the *capital*. The shaft, though occasionally octagonal, was usually cylindrical, and was sometimes grooved or banded into complex patterns. Because it stood on a square base, a small leaf or *spur* was carved into the four corners of the latter to 'marry' the two together. On the top sat a square capital – an *abacus* – from which the arch

*Examples of scalloped and volute capitals.*

*The impressive Norman arcade with cushion capitals*
*at Chichester Cathedral, West Sussex.*

*Detail of a scalloped capital.*

would spring. These capitals were carved in simple geometric patterns and are of three types: the *cushion,* the simplest, in which the square stone is merely rounded off to meet the shaft; the *scalloped,* in which the square stone is carved on the lower part in such a way that it resembles the ribs of a scallop shell as it joins the shaft; and the rather more sophisticated *volute,* in which the stone is carved into stylized acanthus leaves – looking a little like a Corinthian capital.

As in so many other instances, the finest workmanship is to be found in the cathedrals, and for the best Norman piers, you must go to Durham. However, having seen those, you will appreciate even more the charm of the parish church piers raised by nameless travelling masons. No cathedral can give you the thrill that you will experience the first time you see the little Norman church at Kilpeck in Herefordshire. The masons who worked there had certainly been influenced by the Scandinavians, and their invention is amazing. Any conversation between ecclesiologists must include some reference to Kilpeck. Old actors used to say, 'Ah – but did you see Henry Irving?' Old politicians used to say, 'Ah – but did you hear Winston Churchill?' Ecclesiologists can still say, 'Ah – but have you seen Kilpeck?'

As you may remember, early parishioners preferred to be buried on the south side of the church, so the north side was the obvious place to build the first extension. However, if there were still not enough room for the congregation, they had no alternative but to repeat the extension on the south side. We soon had north and south aisles joined to the nave by arcades composed of bays. These aisles were not only to accommodate the growing population but also to provide an alternative route for the processions used by the priests to dramatize the ritual of the church services, and to provide space for more altars and statues.

*A massive Norman pier with a stylized capital*
*at Rodmell, East Sussex.*

These early builders soon encountered the sort of problem you would find if you were to put an extension immediately outside your sitting-room window: your sitting-room would be very dark. The only way the Normans could overcome this same problem was to increase the height of the nave and put the windows very high up above the roof of the extension. This became the 'clear storey' or, as the experts describe it, *clerestory.* But how do you pronounce 'clerestory'? Not even the experts can agree – some say 'clearstory', some say '*clair*stery' and some say 'cle-*rest*-ary'. I wish they would make up their minds. The Victorians, who virtually invented ecclesiology as a serious study, were very fond of giving strange names to everything, and now we are stuck with them. For instance, the space inside the sloping roof of the extension they named the *triforium*; no one knows why, but it is quite a nice word. You try saying it: 'try-for-ee-umm'.

The window openings in these Norman churches remained very small, but more decoration was used on the frames:

*Norman windows with highly decorated frames, Petersfield, Hampshire.*

*The arcade, triforium and clerestory in the transitional retrochoir*
*at Chichester Cathedral, West Sussex.*

The same series of mouldings that we have noted on the doors were used to frame the windows.

The towers became larger and larger, and looked more like the keeps of castles, except in certain areas where there was a shortage of stone, mainly in south-east England. In these areas, the Normans often built circular towers of flint and rubble – circular because having no corners, no large stones were needed. Jolly clever. Where delivery could be effected by boats navigating the rivers in this part of England, the Normans imported enormous quantities of stone from Caen in northern France, but stone was in plentiful supply in the rest of the country. A great belt of limestone runs right across the country from Dorset to Yorkshire, and most of our churches are built of this wonderfully durable material. Further west, the limestone is of a beautiful honey colour.

Another invention of the Normans was the *blind arcade*. This was a series of plain or interlaced arches built into the walls either inside or outside. As well as being extremely decorative, they helped to bond together the rubble walling.

*Norman turret with blind arcading, Christchurch Priory, Dorset.*

Here I must underline the fact that all these changes in church architecture didn't suddenly find favour all over England in one day. The wealthy monasteries and abbeys were continually expanding, building and rebuilding, and they employed the finest master masons, many of whom were teeming with ideas. If these were acceptable to their patrons, they were soon copied across the country, but the further the community was from one of the few cities or religious centres, the longer it took.

These master masons were the forerunners of the architects of today. For many years, it was thought that the great medieval buildings happened almost by accident in the hands of itinerant stone cutters, but modern scholarship has been able to detect the imprint of brilliant individuals on various buildings. Now we even know the names of many of these men, the greatest of whom was Henry Yevele whose finest work can be seen at Westminster Abbey.

The master mason was responsible for the overall design, while the work was actually carried out by 'freemasons' who were the contractors. Their site offices were called 'lodges', and there they supervised the stone cutters and carvers. Their skills were jealously guarded and were imparted in strict secrecy: each degree of expertise was marked by a ceremony, the details of which were known only to those who had reached that degree. When a mason, stone cutter or apprentice moved on to his next job, his new employer would understand from secret signs, such as a handshake, just how qualified he might be. The fact that we know so little about these craftsmen is due to the secrecy in which they surrounded themselves: even the details of their plans were incised into plaster so that they could be reduced to rubble the moment they had served their purpose. Remarkably, a section of one of these tracings can be glimpsed above the porch of Wells Cathedral.

We like to think that high-rise buildings, which first appeared in London in the 1960s and then spread like a disease across the country to ruin our cities, were spawned by the skyscrapers of New York, but in San Gimignano in Italy, scores of tower blocks were built in the 13th century. Nothing is new. So local church builders of the Middle Ages incorporated any of the new ideas they could persuade their patrons to accept – just as you would if you were to build yourself a house: do you or do you not want a conservatory or a jacuzzi?

# The Early English Style

Some time towards the end of the 12th century, something astonishing happened. Someone – we don't know who – invented a brilliant solution to a problem. The problem had been apparent for centuries, especially in the larger ecclesiastical buildings which had vaulted stone ceilings. Norman vaults, like their arches, were semi-circular, and if transepts were erected at right angles to the nave, the vaults joined quite happily as long as the height and width of the transept were the same as those of the nave.

You don't have to know a lot about geometry to appreciate that the height of a semi-circular arch must be equal to half its span/width, so if the height of the nave and the transepts were the same, but the nave was wider, the cross vaulting would be impossible structurally and aesthetically – one would be a perfect semi-circle and the other would be squashed. A great problem . . .

Then this nameless person thought, 'Why does an arch have to be semi-circular? If I knock out the horizontal lintel of a door, the wall above will always fall away in an equilateral triangle – it will be unstable at points A and B but point C will remain stable – so if I knock out the loose bits at points A and B, I will be left with a pointed arch.' The man was a genius.

*An Early English arch frames a view of Peterborough Cathedral, Cambridgeshire.*

Church building took a new turn and the style known as 'Early English' (the earliest mature type of English Gothic) was born, marked by the new arch and other advanced techniques which allowed the walls to become thinner and taller.

One of these new techniques was the use of buttresses in place of the massive walls on which the Normans had relied entirely for strength. If you put

*Buttresses to the nave at Chichester Cathedral, West Sussex.*

a flat roof on a building, the weight is carried directly by the walls, and if the roof is too heavy, the walls will be crushed. However, if you put on a sloping roof, the weight of it is always pushing the walls outward, even if you try to hold them together with a series of tie beams. Imagine that you are standing in front of a tall cupboard which begins to fall towards you: you wouldn't try to hold it up at floor level; you would immediately put one foot behind the other and brace yourself by placing both your hands as high up on the cupboard as possible. If you could then see yourself sideways in a mirror, you would see that you are doing exactly what a buttress does when it prevents a wall from being pushed over. The new church builders discovered that if they placed buttresses *outside* the church to support the outward thrust of the roof, the walls could be thinner and more space could be used for windows.

The new tall windows are called *lancet* because of their lance-like shape and it was not long before several were grouped together – in threes, fives or sevens – to make virtually one window framed by a single pointed arch which, on the outside, formed a hood-mould – called a *dripstone* – to divert the rain from running down the glass.

*Lancet windows of the Early English period.*

*Graceful Early English shafts made from Purpeck Marble.*

The massive cylindrical shafts of the Norman piers gave way to dignified columns, quite often comprising tall slender shafts surrounding a central member, their combined strength equalling that of a single large pier. The outer shafts were frequently made from the darker Purbeck marble, thus adding another decorative feature.

The capitals and bases which in Norman architecture were mainly square, now began to echo the shape of the shafts, and as the stone carvers became more expert, they bravely used their chisels to undercut the stone, thus throwing their carvings into high relief. Two new types of capital evolved. One was carved with stylized leaves – for which the Victorians invented a phrase, *still-leaf foliage*, which I suppose is quite logical. The other was in the shape of an inverted bell and looks as if it had been turned on a lathe; this became known as a *bell capital* – again logical.

New Shoreham Church.
A.C.F. 1913

Capitals carved with still-leaf foliage support the
arch on the left, New Shoreham church, West Sussex.

*Salisbury Cathedral, Wiltshire, possibly the finest
example of Early English architecture.*

*Mouldings at the base
of an Early English pier.*

The bases of the piers were moulded, and incorporated a new shape: a deeply undercut hollow between the rolls of mouldings.

The masons of the Early English period also invented a new decoration for their mouldings which is known as *dog tooth*, again I can't think why because I've never seen a dog's tooth that looks anything like it. However, you can see row upon row of these dog's teeth around the windows, doors and arches constructed at this time.

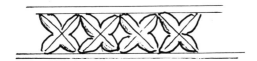

*Dog tooth decoration.*

If you get a chance, go to see Salisbury Cathedral. Most of our cathedrals have evolved over centuries and contain many different architectural styles, but Salisbury was built all in one go – starting in the year 1220, and as a result, it is probably the best example of the Early English style. Victorian architects thought this the purest of all medieval styles and studiously copied the details from Salisbury in their own churches, which sprang up all over the country in the mid-19th-century Gothic Revival.

HARDHAM PRIORY
1909.

*Windows from the Decorated period with*
*geometric tracery.*

# The
# Decorated Style

As every schoolchild knows, the Norman invasion took place in 1066. Their style of architecture lasted almost exactly 100 years, so it can be said that the use of the pointed arch and the resulting Early English style began in about 1166. I must reiterate that all these new ideas were not incorporated all over the country in one night. After the inception of a new idea – in, say, Canterbury – it might take thirty years before we find it being used in far-flung areas.

Strangely enough, and conveniently for us, the Early English style also lasted for 100 years. However, as the builders and masons became more and more sophisticated, a new style emerged in about 1266: *Decorated*.

The first sign of this was in the design of windows. Someone found that, instead of placing lancet windows in arrangement of odd numbers – ones, threes, fives, sevens – if two were put together side by side under a single pointed arch frame, there was a space between them at the top which could be cut out in decorative shapes such as circles, trefoils or quatrefoils. This is called *plate* or *geometric* tracery.

After the fairly simple discovery of geometric/plate tracery, the masons and their sculptors went raving mad. They cut holes in the tops of windows wherever they could and the stone between the holes got narrower and narrower. They soon found that it was easier to construct these windows with ready-cut stone *mullions* (vertical bars) rather than cutting them from the solid. A simple curve was not good enough: they added *cusps* (pointed projections which, only for decoration's sake, protrude from the curved line and then return), and made lines swoop and rise and dip, so much so that it became known as *curvilinear* tracery.

They even succeeded in carving the stonework of a window in the shape of a stylized family tree showing the genealogy of Christ from the root of Jesse (the father of King David). Logically, these are known as 'Jesse windows'.

It was all wonderfully exciting. They made their windows larger and larger and filled the spaces between the mullions with stained glass. The Normans had painted their stonework in brightly coloured patterns, but now the sunlight could filter through the great coloured windows and play across the

*Curvilinear tracery in the eastern windows
of two different churches.*

*The pinnacles on the church tower at Sarum, Wiltshire,
lavishly decorated with crockets.*

superb carvings with which the new generation of sculptors filled their
churches. They carved everything in sight – every gable and pinnacle was
covered with the small ornaments (usually a bud or curled leaf) known as
*crockets* and they invented a new ornament called a *ballflower*

*Ballflower decoration.*

which completely took over from the old dog tooth and soon was racing along the mouldings of windows and arches, up every spire and pinnacle, and around the great tombs which were sculpted for wealthy patrons who lay immortalized in beautiful effigies under graceful canopies.

Not to be outdone, the masons developed the art of vaulting. Instead of the severe ribbed vaults of the previous century, they added many more intersecting ribs to produce intricate star-like patterns – called *stellar* vaulting. They even invented a totally new arch (comprising a double continuous curve, concave below and convex above), extremely decorative if not exactly load bearing, known as an *ogee*. (What a ridiculous name for such an elegant device. It sounds like an American expletive.)

*Decorative ogee arches.*

These elegant lines were immediately surrounded by the carvers with crockets, cusps and ballflowers.

One element that the sculptors could not improve upon or embellish were the new columns. As the walls were becoming thinner, the main vertical strength lay in these. While retaining the appearance of the detached slender shafts of the previous century, the masons now fused all the shafts together so that they could be cut from single stones, and they added a new detail known as a *fillet* – a narrow flat projection running up the outer face of a shaft. Alternatively, they constructed the shafts so that, in cross-section, they were octagonal, with octagonal bases and capitals.

Roofs – I do wish we could say rooves: the plural of 'hoof' is 'hooves' so why isn't 'rooves' the plural of 'roof'? However – roofs in the Norman and Early English periods were steeply sloped to allow the rainwater to run off quickly the covering of thatch or the tiles made of wood (called *shingles*), but in the Decorated period, they discovered the advantages of lead, which could make roofs wonderfully watertight. However, lead is also very soft, and if laid on a steep roof, the very weight of it tears it away from its fixings. The answer was to flatten the pitch of the roof considerably. Quite often you can see the outline on the side of a tower of an earlier steep pitch of a nave roof above the present roof line.

*Broach spire at Buxted, East Sussex. Note the little*
*'half pyramid' of roofing.*

Buttresses, too, assumed a new appearance. Norman walls were so thick that, if they were used at all, buttresses served no structural purpose and were purely decorative. Early English ones were solidly built and functional, and were usually topped with a little roof to shed rainwater. Now the masons realized that width was unimportant: it was the amount of projection from the wall that was all important. If an attractive *pinnacle* were placed on the top, the extra weight helped to anchor the buttress to the ground. Of course, they then added crockets to the pinnacle.

During this period, spires rising from towers came into their own. The Normans topped their towers with squat pyramids, but the rainwater collected in the gulleys, so in the next period, the builders carried the roof line over the sides of the tower. Then they complicated the issue by raising octagonal spires

*A squat pyramidical roof on top of a Norman tower.*

*Roof line projecting over the sides of the tower at*
*Shoreham-by-Sea, West Sussex.*

which meant either adding a half pyramid of roofing to each corner of the
square tower or inserting a kind of gusset to effect a happy join to the octagon.
Known as 'broach spires', these created a new problem: if repairs had to be
carried out to the spire, it was necessary to erect scaffolding right up from the
ground which was an expensive, difficult and hazardous business. So in the
Decorated period, they reverted to the old idea of placing the spire inside the
tower parapet (on which scaffolding could be erected), and got rid of the
rainwater through little spouts cut through the parapet.

The spires grew taller and taller and more and more elegant. Some were surfaced with wooden shingles, or with lead in small sections, joined in decorative rolls. However, the better ones were built entirely of stone, with a series of gabled windows which became smaller as they neared the top. And the gables and ridges were again covered with crockets.

Above: *Tall, elegant spires of the Decorated period.*
Above left: *Broach spire with 'gusset'.*
Below left: *Church tower with spire placed inside the parapet.*

The new Decorated fashion swept across the country, albeit taking a number of years to do so. As a consequence, any enlargement of an old church had to be in the new style. Small windows in the walls were knocked out, and large new ones, filled with stained glass, were inserted. If the church had no spire, now was the time to build one stepped with crockets.

# The
# Perpendicular Style

You should have no difficulty remembering the few dates I have given you so far: 1066 or thereabouts is the beginning of the *Norman* period; 1166 or thereabouts is the beginning of *Early English*; 1266 or thereabouts is the beginning of *Decorated*. However, now we come to a more difficult one – 1348 precisely.

In 1348, a terrible plague, known as the Black Death, arrived in England after devastating Europe. The death rate was appalling, especially in the cities: in London alone, they were burying 200 victims every day. At that time, the population of England was approximately 2 million (which seems unimaginable when today it is about 60 million). When the Black Death had run its course, England had lost something like a third of its population – more than 650,000 men, women and children. You stood a much better chance of survival if, for instance, you were an isolated farm worker, but if your work brought you into contact with many other people, your chances were slim.

During the Decorated period, specialized workshops had been created in the major cities where the expert stone carvers turned out their splendid work to order. No longer did they have to travel the country picking up their jobs if and when they could. The orders came to them, they carved the stone which was then delivered to the site in pieces and assembled by lesser craftsmen under the supervision of the master mason. That is why we can see the work of individual sculptors in churches far and wide, even though they were built at the same time. However, in 1348, because of their residence in the cities, hundreds of these skilled craftsmen died – the very men who had been glorifying our churches.

When the country recovered, the construction of churches began again, but without the former exuberance. The architects and masons had to dream up new ideas, ideas that would beautify a building without the help of stone carving, simply because so many of the carvers had died. They hit upon a splendid expedient, and their results became known as the *Perpendicular* style. Their buildings would rely for their strength entirely on the simple device of placing one stone on top of another. No tortured curves, just straight, vertical – *perpendicular* – lines.

*Enormous Perpendicular windows and flying buttresses.*

You may have seen modern steel-framed buildings being erected: Great steel girders are bolted or welded together and these form the total strength of the building. When this stage has been completed, the floors, wall and ceilings (which can be as thin as regulations allow) are fitted in. The churches of the Perpendicular period foreshadowed this method almost exactly: all the strength was in the piers and buttresses, leaving all the spaces in between for purely decorative, non-structural features. With vertical mullions strengthened by horizontal *transoms*, the windows could be made enormous, and the spaces between the windows are so slight that we wonder how the walls can possible stand.

*A splendid Perpendicular window, far left,*
*in the ruins of Kenilworth Castle,*
*Warwickshire.*

The builders also invented a new type of arch, which was not very practical but, with more and more windows and thinner walls, there was less weight for the arches to carry. It looks a little as if someone has sat on the point of an Early English arch and squashed it. These arches were frequently set in a square-headed frame. The flat panels of the masonry were decorated – if you can call it that – with simple cusps, circles and heraldic coats of arms. One idea that was carried over from the Decorated period was the use of a continuous moulding, which ran right from the base of the arch and round, uninterrupted by capitals, to the base of the other side.

The Perpendicular style first erupted at Gloucester. Edward II had been murdered at Berkeley Castle in 1327, and his body was brought to rest in Gloucester, in what is now the cathedral. This was not a purely pious act by the monks: the very presence of the body of a martyr or a monarch in a church would immediately result in a vast influx of pilgrims who would pay to be fed and housed. These same pilgrims would be expected to make large donations to the monastery and to purchase mementoes and souvenirs, all of which ensured extremely good profits for the monks. (The nearest thing we have today is the vast tourist industry surrounding the birthplace and grave of Shakespeare.)

*Perpendicular doorway with a square-headed hood mould,*
*Cowdray Park, Midhurst, West Sussex.*

Perpendicular doorway almost hidden by a covered font
in the foreground.

Canterbury was at the top of this league: not only was it the Christian capital of England, but the Archbishop, Thomas à Becket, was murdered in that very church in 1170 at the behest of none other than the king, Henry II. Becket was buried there, and was almost immediately proclaimed a martyr. A vast jewel-encrusted shrine was erected, and every Christian in England was expected to make the pilgrimage to his tomb – and to pay handsomely for the privilege. First Lindisfarne and then Durham had St Cuthbert, Chichester had St Richard, Winchester had King William II – known as William Rufus (son of William the Conqueror), Worcester had King John and then, not to be outdone, Gloucester got Edward II. The pilgrims arrived in their thousands – and so did their donations.

When sufficient funds had accumulated, the top priority for the monks was to beautify the grim gaunt Norman chancel where Edward's body was buried. This had been built with massive piers supporting a massive triforium, which was topped by a massive clerestory, and to demolish it would have been almost impossible, especially when the Black Death intervened. The monks and their master builder hit upon a brilliant solution: a network of masonry finely cut in vertical lines would be appliquéd to the surface of the Norman stonework. The resulting effect is rather like hanging a bead curtain over a doorway: at first sight, you see only the curtain, but after careful inspection, you can see the archway behind it. The Perpendicular style was born.

For many years, the middle classes had been growing in importance and they now began to make their presence felt in the churches. Wealthy families built their own chapels within them and provided endowments to pay for priests who then would sing (or chant) daily Masses for the souls of a particular family's dead relatives. These are known as *chantry chapels*.

Also at this time, skilled workmen had formed themselves into guilds and frequently paid for a church to be enlarged to incorporate their guild chapel. This was usually done by extending the aisles at the eastern ends parallel with the chancel.

With the lack of carved stone ornament, the Perpendicular churches were in danger of appearing rather bare, but a great bonus was to hand. For centuries, the masons and sculptors had had church building virtually to themselves, but now the carpenters and joiners came into their own and proved themselves equal to the challenge. Their invention and craftsmanship was astonishing. The joiners constructed and carved magnificent choir screens and choir stalls and the carpenters invented the glorious *Hammerbeam* roof. The braces of this were often carved with angels – you can almost hear the flutter of their wings.

Not to be outdone the masons went one better and invented the *fan vault* – the most spectacular of all. Take an opened fan in one hand, firmly depress the centre with your thumb and hold it up at arms length. Your arm will represent the shaft, and the ribs and web of the fan will represent the new vault, which first appeared in the cloister at Gloucester and can be seen to stunning effect in

King's College Chapel at Cambridge and in the Henry VII Chapel at Westminster Abbey. Looking upwards at these light, gossamer vaults, one can hardly believe that they are made of stone: surely they must be papier mâche. Very few parish churches have them, but they are well worth searching for.

Towards the end of the 14th century a scholar, John Wycliffe, sowed the seeds for a liturgical revolution that was to echo down the centuries. I don't intend to delve into the minutiae of his theology and politics, but they coincided with a great desire of a growing number of the laity to understand the teachings of the Bible for themselves. No longer were they content to sit back passively, making automatic responses as the priest intoned in Latin from the confines of the sanctuary. Wycliffe translated the Bible into English, but the ecclesiastical authorities objected and proclaimed that even the possession of an English Bible was the sign of heresy.

However, the movement resulted in the introduction of the sermon into church services whereby the priests could interpret the Bible to their flock. Very soon, every church had to have a pulpit – a raised platform from which the priest could be seen and heard. Portable pulpits of some type had been used for centuries, but now pulpits made of wood or stone became permanent fixtures, set in the nave near the chancel arch and often attached for support to one of the columns. For some inexplicable reason, they are usually octagonal, and many are splendidly ornate. Quite soon *testers* were added – canopies made of wood, which would reflect the voice of the preacher which might otherwise fade away into the rafters.

Thus elevated, the preacher required an attentive audience. Hitherto, the congregation had either stood or knelt throughout a service, but now they began to be provided with permanent seating in the form of benches. The earliest of these were plain oak planks between two plain solid ends, which of course the wood carvers soon found irresistible. Again, we find geographical differences: the carvers in the south-west of England left the bench ends as rectangular panels which they covered with inventive patterns and emblems; while the carvers in the rest of the country elongated the bench ends into pinnacles or 'poppyheads', a name which some writers say is derived from the French word *poupee*, meaning a bunch of hemp or flax, while others say that it is from the Latin *puppis*, meaning the figurehead of a ship. Either way, these decorative bench ends are some of the glories of the Perpendicular period.

Perpendicular remained the style until the Reformation began in 1534. (We don't often remember that all our churches were Roman Catholic until then.) With the Reformation, medieval Gothic building came to an end.

# The
# English Reformation

If only Henry VIII had not married Katherine of Aragon, England in the years that followed might have been a happier place. Katherine had been betrothed as a 12-year-old to Henry's elder brother, Arthur, who was one year younger, and they were married four years later. She always maintained that the marriage had not been consummated and when Arthur died less than five months after their wedding, she was allowed by the Pope to marry his brother, Henry, the new heir to the throne. During the years of their life together, Katherine produced many children, all of whom either died at birth or shortly after, except for one daughter, Mary, who thus became heir to the throne. It grieved Henry that he had no son to carry on his line, so he determined to set Katherine aside and marry again.

But how to do it? The Roman Catholic Church would not countenance a divorce, so perhaps an annulment (on the grounds that his entire marriage to Katherine, his brother's widow, was invalid in the eyes of God) would be acceptable? A bit late after eighteen years!

Ecclesiastics from all over Christendom argued about it for years. One side maintained that a marriage is a marriage once you have 'taken a wife', while the other maintained that a marriage is only a marriage when it is consummated. Two quotations from the Bible became instrumental in the argument. The Book of Leviticus states: 'You shall not uncover the nakedness of your brother's wife: she is your brother's nakedness . . . If a man takes his brother's wife, it is impurity: he has uncovered his brother's nakedness; they shall be childless.' The Book of Deuteronomy states: 'If brothers dwell together, and one of them dies and has no son, the wife of the dead shall not be married outside the family to a stranger: her husband's brother shall go in to her, and take her as his wife.'

Henry, of course, took the side that would suit him best, but the Pope took the other. There was a stalemate until Henry took advantage of the Reformation then gaining ground in Europe and made himself ' Supreme Head of the Church in England' in 1531 and had the Archbishop of Canterbury declare his marriage to Katherine void in 1533. Three months before, he had secretly married Anne Boleyn, who just had time to give birth to Elizabeth before having her head chopped off so that Henry could marry the third of his six wives, Jane Seymour, who died while giving birth to his longed-for son, Edward.

As Supreme Head of the Church of England, Henry set about the destruction of the monasteries which, by this time, owned approximately a quarter of all the land in England, but for a time the parish churches were safe. At long last, a translation of the Bible into English was officially sanctioned, which appeared in 1539 – every church was to provide one for all to read, if they could read!

Henry VIII died in 1547 and his son, Edward VI, succeeded to the throne at the age of 9. His advisers were fiercely committed to reform of the church, and a directive went out that everything 'corrupt, vain and superstitious' in the parish churches should be destroyed. As a result, altars were removed and replaced by wooden Communion tables, paintings were obliterated, statues broken, glass smashed, and shrines erected over the bodies of saints were removed. The only thing for which we can thank Edward and his advisers is the introduction of the superb Book of Common Prayer. Within six years, Edward was dead and the throne went to Catherine's daughter, the staunchly Catholic Mary, who made herself extremely unpopular by burning a number of Protestant martyrs in an attempt to bring England back under the yoke of Rome. It was a yoke that most Englishmen did not find funny.

For a few brief years, England became once again an officially Roman Catholic country, until the accession of Elizabeth I, who reasserted the Act of Supremacy, thus making herself – like her father and half-brother – Supreme Head of the Church in England. But Elizabeth inherited a deeply divided population: the majority were happy to accept the doctrines of the Church of England, but on either side were the deeply committed Roman Catholics and the new Protestant idealists, known as Puritans. These two groups became the 'outsiders', and many of them later set sail to find religious tolerance in America.

These troubled decades were not the best of times in which to build churches.

# The
# Palladian Style

James I of England and VI of Scotland succeeded Elizabeth in 1603, and it was in his reign that the next great leap forward in architecture occurred. That great patron of the arts, the formidable Thomas Howard, Earl of Arundel, embarked on a tour of Italy at the beginning of the century, and took with him a young artist named Inigo Jones. Jones was captivated by the work of two Italian architects who had based their theories and designs on the architecture of ancient Rome – Andrea Palladio and his pupil Vincenzo Scamozzi. They and other contemporary Italian architects had drawn heavily on the published works of the ancient Roman master, Vitruvius, who had defined the 'orders' of classical architecture: the Greek orders of *Doric*, *Ionic* and *Corinthian*; and he added two more, *Tuscan* and *Composite*. Whole books have been written describing the details of the orders so it is unnecessary for me to try to do so here.

Immediately after his return to England, Inigo Jones was commissioned by James I to design the Queen's House at Greenwich. Fortunately, this building can still be seen, framed like a jewel by later buildings designed by Wren, Hawksmoor and Gibbs. Just imagine the shock to the people of London, accustomed as they were to timber-framed houses with each floor overhanging the one below, when they saw the clean lines of the stone walls and harmoniously placed windows and doors of the Queen's House. Jones' next commission was to erect a private chapel beside St James's Palace, and here he incorporated the first 'Venetian' window to be seen in England – a tall central window with a semi-circular head and, on each side, a shorter window with a square head.

However, the 'great leap' that concerns us here occurred in 1631. The part of London now known as Covent Garden was owned by the Earl of Bedford. He decided to build a piazza in the Italian style, dominated on its western end by a church – and who better than Inigo Jones to design the whole thing? The Earl was no great churchman and merely wanted the church to provide a focal point; he stipulated that it was not to be much better than a barn, to which Jones is reputed to have replied, 'You shall have the handsomest barn in England.'

Sadly, the piazza itself is no longer as Jones designed it, but the church – St

Paul's, Covent Garden – is still there with its massive, deeply recessed pediment supported by four equally massive Tuscan columns. What appears to be the central doorway is in fact a deception: immediately behind it stands the high altar in the traditional position in the east. The main entrance is, in fact, at the other end, set in a delightful tree-studded garden. The interior is a large and spacious box, lit by tall, semi-circular-headed windows of plain glass.

If the Queen's House had been a shock to Londoners what must they have thought of St Paul's? Previously they had known only churches built in the Gothic style with towers, spires, pinnacles, crockets and pointed windows. Suddenly they were presented with a totally new architectural concept; for which Jones had used, for the first time, a white stone from Portland. The next time you are in London, please go along to St Paul's, Covent Garden, close your eyes, remember your own nearest Gothic church, then open your eyes and experience the same thrill that the average Londoner felt in 1633 when he saw this church on the day it was opened.

I have a particular affection for St Paul's because it is the 'Actors Church'. Standing as it does in the centre of theatreland, actors have worshipped here since it was built. It is here that services are held to give thanks for the lives of departed performers, many of whom are remembered by plaques on the surrounding walls. During her long life, the 'Queen Mother' of the British theatre, Dame Sybil Thorndike, attended many of these memorial services. After being greeted fondly by friends and admirers as she left the west door following one of them, she exclaimed as she was helped into the waiting car, 'Wasn't that *fun*! When is the next one?'

James I's son and heir, Charles I, rather lost his head in Whitehall – incidently, outside the Banqueting Hall, also designed by Inigo Jones – and then followed the Interregnum. A disastrous time for church furnishings. Cromwell's Puritan troops were ordered to remove or deface all things of an idolatrous or superstitious nature, and they went about it more venomously than had the men under Edward VI's advisers – they even used guns to remove parts that could not be reached any other way.

There was, however, an important gain during these years and for some time afterwards. Dissenting chapels sprang up all over the country, and their cool, bare interiors are delightful. The focal point is not the altar but the pulpit, and there are plain walls and clear glass windows – nothing to distract the congregation from listening to the words of the Bible or the sermon. Box pews were installed, each with its own door to keep out the draughts. These beautiful buildings are a study in themselves: the Meeting House, in Ditchling, East Sussex, is a delightful example.

# Neo-Classicism
# and Baroque

The year 1666, shortly after the Restoration of Charles II to the throne, was marked by the Great Fire of London. (I have recently had the pleasure of reading all nine volumes of Samuel Pepys's *Diary*, which covers in fascinating detail the whole of this period.) We are told that eighty-four parish churches were destroyed in that conflagration. Fortuitously, an architect of genius was to hand to cope with the rebuilding: Christopher Wren.

Wren first planned to rebuild the City almost completely, beginning by driving new thoroughfares in straight lines radiating from a rebuilt St Paul's Cathedral, but vested interest prevented him, so he was constrained into building fifty-one new churches on restricted sites. His invention was phenomenal. He knew that, due to lack of space, the outer walls would hardly ever be seen, so he concentrated his efforts on the interiors and on the spires.

Nearly all of Wren's churches are rectangular in plan, and as this was the beginning of the age of the sermon, pride of place was given to the pulpit. While still adhering to classical orders, Wren used the new freedom which had evolved from the academic principles of Inigo Jones, and which led to the style that followed: *baroque*. Ornate plaster ceilings picked out in gold, walls and galleries decorated with swags, cartouches and emblems carved in wood or plaster, all provide endless joyous delights for the eye.

And as for Wren's spires, who would have believed that the straight-sided Gothic version could be developed with such infinite variety? The view of London from the top of Southwark Cathedral became a forest of spires – no two alike – and the view was crowned by Wren's masterpiece, St Paul's Cathedral. It is difficult to appreciate as we look at that skyline now, overwhelmed as it is by tower blocks of miserable concrete, that at the time of the construction of St Paul's there was a law that banned any building over five stories high (would that this law still existed!). Aware of this, Wren planned the main body of St Paul's in two strongly demarcated horizontal sections, the lower half of each in the Ionic order and the upper in Corinthian. The lower half was the height of a five-storey house so that, when viewed from a distance, the upper half surmounted by the beautiful drum and dome appears to be the complete cathedral floating on the surrounding roofs.

While on the subject of rules and regulations, there is currently a campaign seeking to ensure that a percentage of the cost of any new building must be devoted to works of art to be incorporated into the design. Laudable as this may seem, time was when buildings themselves were works of art. What would Wren have said if the authorities had insisted that a 'work of art' had to be stuck on to St Paul's?

As it is, the inscription on Wren's own simple tomb in the crypt of St Paul's says it all: 'SI MONUMENTUM REQUIRIS, CIRCUMSPICE.' ('If you require a monument, look about you.') A visit to St Paul's is not complete until you visit that tomb and reflect on the inscription.

You may notice that baptismal fonts became much smaller at this time. This is because the Church of England decreed that total immersion was no longer necessary: a symbolic wetting of a baby's head and a simple sign of the cross made by the priest with holy water was all that was required. (This, of course, was not accepted by the strict Baptists.) In addition, stone altars were replaced by communion tables, and where once an elaborate ornamental screen called a *reredos* panelled the wall behind the altar, now large boards took its place, on which the Ten Commandments, the Creed and the Lord's Prayer were written – all in English.

Also at this time it became possible to tune bells accurately, so instead of the discordant ringing of disparate bells – albeit an attractive sound, as can still be heard in Italy – parishioners could now ring 'changes' on the bells. Ringing chambers were installed in church towers and the art of campinology was born – an art in which the English still lead the world.

Christoper Wren was followed by two great architects in the baroque style: Nicholas Hawksmoor and James Gibbs, both of whose work was copied all over England and later (especially Gibbs) in America. Hawksmoor had for years laboured under the shadow of Sir John Vanbrugh – an architect known mainly for his great houses such as Blenheim Palace in Oxfordshire, Castle Howard in North Yorkshire and Seaton Delaval Hall in Northumberland – and only very recently has his due merit been recognized. Hawksmoor's masterpieces in London are St George's in Bloomsbury and Christchurch, Spitalfields. Gibbs designed (again, both in London) St Mary-le-Strand and St Martin-in-the-Fields, where he shocked the purists by placing a spire immediately above a classical pediment! Previously spires had risen from their own towers, and pediments had never been topped by anything. Whatever the purists thought – and many still think the same – this combination found great favour in the New World.

# The
# 18th Century to
# the Present

By the middle of the 18th century, architects, lead by Colen Campbell, returned to the basic principles of Palladio, but the great era of post-Commonwealth church building was over – for the time being. Most villages and towns already had their churches, and the people with money to spare preferred to embellish their own houses.

Architects seem to have run out of original ideas, and were continually looking to the past for inspiration. Greece had been under the domination of Turkey for many years, and during their brave battles leading to independence in 1830, all things Greek became fashionable in the Western world. Although Roman architecture had been heavily based on the Greek example, Western architects had not, until this time, looked back to the source of the classical orders. Suddenly everyone wanted buildings in the Greek style – well, almost everyone. At the same time, some architects thought that pagan architecture was inappropriate for Christian buildings, and looked back to what they considered the English national style – Gothic. The result, of course, was that the beginning of the 19th century saw buildings of all styles springing up: Greek, Roman, Gothic – even Indian, Egyptian and Chinese!

In the Greek style, John Nash gave us All Souls, Langham Place in London, and William and Henry Inwood (father and son) designed or, rather, slavishly copied the porch of the Erechtheion on Athen's Acropolis at St Pancras, Euston Road, also in London, while the young Charles Barry provided St Peter's, Brighton, in the Gothic. However, the great champion of the Gothic was Augustus Pugin and he and Barry set about the rebuilding of the Houses of Parliament in the form that can still be seen today. Their work coincided with the formation of the Oxford Movement, as well as the Cambridge Camden Society (later known as the Ecclesiological Society) who maintained that the perfect Gothic style was the Decorated, and that the interiors of churches must be just as those of that period: the altar must once again be the focal point; therefore, the pulpit was pushed to one side, with a lectern on the other.

Suddenly there erupted on to the architectural stage George Gilbert Scott (best known, I suppose, for the Albert Memorial). He designed hundreds of churches all over England, and 'restored' hundreds more, but he often swept away superb things that had been added in intervening periods.

During the Industrial Revolution, a large proportion of the population moved into the new industrial centres. Consequently, most of the ecclesiastical buildings of the 19th century are to be seen in such towns. Most of them were built at the personal expense of the newly rich industrialists, and one such, Edward Akroyd, commissioned Gilbert Scott to design All Souls' in Halifax. Money appeared to be no obstacle, and Scott raised a vast impressive structure topped by a great spire. On one occasion, I was seated in a pew contemplating the magnificent interior of this church when I noticed something strange. On the back of the pew in front of me was a long shelf to hold the required prayer and hymn books but beneath it were two strips of wood, 11 inches apart, which formed a slot. In cross-section, the strips looked like a piece of picture frame.

Were these runners supposed to hold a now-vanished drawer? I looked along the pew and noticed many more pairs: one in front of each alternate seat. All the other pews had similar pairs of runners. Then I noticed that in each pew the first pair was in front of the seat nearest the aisle, then a space, then another pair and so on. Suddenly, I knew the answer. In these Victorian mill towns, the men would wear their best black suits to go to church, and the customary accessory was a bowler-hat, the brim of which perfectly slotted in to the runners. The man was seated on the outside, then a woman (no slot required), then another man, then a woman and so on. How ingenious!

Very few churches have been built in the 20th century, and most of them are, I think, disasters – especially Coventry Cathedral. The decision had been made to leave the ruins of the bombed cathedral as a monument – with a cross made form charred beams on the altar and the heart-rending, but heartening, inscription below: 'Father Forgive' – and to build the new post-war cathedral at right angles on a north-south axis. The south wall is a wall of engraved glass. Inside, as you approach the altar, there is not a window to be seen as they are in slits, set at an angle rising the whole height of the church. The idea is that, as you turn after receiving Communion, you should see, for the first time, the Light coming through the stained glass. In practice, you are blinded by the sunlight blasted at you through the great southern glass wall.

Only two things please me at Coventry: the splendid baptistry window by John Piper and Jacob Epstein's bronzes of *St Michael and the Devil* on the outer wall. I have spent hours trying to work out the geometric pattern of circles and triangles on which his sculpture is based.

I apologize for airing my prejudices, but I believe my grandfather was more prejudiced against modern architecture than I: I can find nothing in his vast collection of drawings of any building erected after 1538!

# Part Two
# A Typical English Parish Church

*A typical parish church with its enclosed churchyard,*
*West Chiltington, West Sussex.*

# The
# Parish Church

So much for the styles – Saxon, Norman, Early English, Decorated, Perpendicular, Palladian, Baroque, Greek, Gothic Revival and so on. Only very occasionally do we find a parish church that was totally completed during the years when any one particular style held sway, so that the architecture is 'pure'. That is the fascination of ecclesiology – discovering which different styles comprise a church is like unravelling a complex detective story. Let us take a close look at what would be a typical church, with a mixture of styles.

The churchyard is enclosed by a fence or a wall and the entrance is through a gate with a roof above it. Prior to an interment, this is where the coffin could rest, protected to some extent from the weather, to await the arrival of the priest. It is called a 'lych-gate' from the Old English word *lic* meaning 'corpse'.

Once inside the churchyard, we almost invariably will see some yew trees. The theory is that yews were originally planted in churchyards many hundreds of years ago, to provide England's longbowmen with the best wood from which their bows could be made. An alternative theory is that since the leaves of the yew are poisonous and it would be certain death to domestic animals if they ate them, priests had yews planted in churchyards to force local farmers to protect their stock by keeping the churchyard fencing secure at their expense rather than that of the church!

Around us will be a forest of tombstones, the oldest on the south side and nearest to the church because parishioners then were superstitious and afraid of a shadow being cast on their graves. Only very rarely can we find a stone dating before the year 1700. Many of the 18th-century stones are adorned with extremely beautiful carving – for example, the winged heads of cherubs and skulls of scythes symbolizing death. In the iron-smelting districts of the Weald of Sussex and Kent, there are many tombstones of cast iron.

*The lych-gate at the entrance to the churchyard at*
*Bidborough, Kent.*

*Intricately carved 18th-century tombstones.*

*Table tombs situated close to the church door at*
*Ardingly, Sussex.*

The most important and wealthy local dignitaries were buried inside the church, as near as possible to the altar, but if they didn't quite merit this honour, their families erected table tombs, which look like large rectangular boxes, outside in the churchyard.

The nearer they were to the church door, the better – they would be at the front of the queue on the Day of Judgement. The following piece of wisdom is to be found on one tombstone:

> HERE I LIE AT THE CHANCEL DOOR
> HERE I LIE BECAUSE I'M POOR
> THE FURTHER IN THE MORE YOU PAY
> HERE I LIE AS WARM AS THEY.

Searching for interesting inscriptions is very rewarding. Here are three I found recently at St Mary's church in Bury St Edmunds:

> SARAH YE WIFE OF ED WORTON
> DYED YE 7 OF NOV 1698 AGED 69
>
> GOOD PEOPLE ALL AS YOU PASS BY
> LOOKE ROUND, SEE HOW CORPSES DO LYE,
> FOR AS YOU ARE SOME TIME WERE WE
> AND AS WE ARE SO MUST YOU BE

> HERE LIES INTERRED THE BODY OF
> MARY HASELTON
> A YOUNG MAIDEN OF THIS TOWN
> BORN OF ROMAN CATHOLIC PARENTS
> AND VIRTUOUSLY BROUGHT UP
> WHO BEING IN THE ACT OF PRAYER
> REPEATING HER VESPERS
> WAS INSTANTANEOUSLY KILLED BY A FLASH
> OF LIGHTNING. AUG 16 1785
> AGED 9 YEARS

READER
PAUSE AT THIS HUMBLE STONE
IT RECORDS THE FALL OF UNGUARDED YOUTH
BY THE ALLUREMENTS OF VICE
AND THE TREACHEROUS SNARES
OF SEDUCTION
SARAH LLOYD
ON THE 23 OF APRIL 1800
IN THE 22 YEAR OF HER AGE
SUFFERED A JUST BUT IGNOMINIOUS DEATH
FOR ADMITTING HER ABANDONED SEDUCER
INTO THE DWELLING HOUSE OF
HER MISTRESS
IN THE NIGHT OF 3 OCT 1799
AND BECOMING THE INSTRUMENT
IN HIS HAND OF THE CRIMES
OF ROBBERY AND HOUSE BURNING
THESE WERE HER LAST WORDS
MAY MY EXAMPLE BE A
WARNING TO THOUSANDS

You may find the following at St Nicholas' in Brighton:

PHOEBE HESSEL
BORN AT STEPNEY IN THE YEAR 1713
SERVED FOR MANY YEARS AS A PRIVATE
IN THE FIFTH REGIMENT OF FOOT
IN DIFFERENT PARTS OF EUROPE
AND IN THE YEAR 1745
FOUGHT UNDER THE COMMAND OF THE
DUKE OF CUMBERLAND
AT THE BATTLE OF FONTENOY,
WHERE SHE RECEIVED A BAYONET WOUND
IN THE ARM
HER LONG LIFE COMMENCED
IN THE REIGN OF
QUEEN ANNE
AND ENDED IN THE REIGN OF
GEORGE IV
12 DECEMBER 1821
AGED 108 YEARS

*A trio of parishioners' graves at Ditchling, Sussex.*

We will notice that all the graves have their feet towards the east; only the clergy are buried the other way round, facing their congregation even in death. Many new tombstones are made from white Italian marble, which does not harmonize well with the surrounding mellow English stone.

Oh, by the way, you may notice an odd thing as you look round at early tombstones: some of them record 1752/3 as part of the inscription, while others may have a date and the letters OS or NS. The reason for this is wonderfully complicated but fascinating.

The year as we know it begins on the first of January but it was not always thus. Our calendar was first regularized by Julius Caesar in 46 BC, with the year comprising 365 days plus one every fourth year (leap year). This is known as the Julian Calendar. In those days, the year began with March, so April was the second month and so on. This is why the seventh month was called September (from the Latin *septem*, meaning 'seven'), October the eighth month (from the Latin *octo*, meaning 'eight'), November the ninth month (Latin *Novem*, meaning 'nine') and December the tenth month (Latin *decem*, meaning 'ten'). (January was named after Janus, the Roman god of gates and beginnings; and February was so named because of Februa, the purification feast that occurred during this month.)

This Julian system was not entirely satisfactory, so in 1582 Pope Gregory XIII reorganized the calendar roughly to coincide with Christmas and made January the first month. This became known as the Gregorian Calendar, but just to make life more difficult, not all the countries adopted it at once: France, among others, accepted it immediately, but Scotland waited until 1600, England until 1752, and Ireland until 1788. It was not adopted in the Soviet Union until 1918!

*A stone cross might mark the spot where early missionaries held their services.*

*Stocks situated just outside a churchyard wall.*

The changeover from one calendar to another in 1752 caused many problems in almost the same way that many people had difficulty in changing to a metric system of money. A proclamation was made that in order to straighten things out 'the day after 2 September 1752 should be reckoned to be 14 September'. Therefore, children born on 2 September would henceforth be twelve days older than they actually were!

More confusion occurred the following year: people who died in January or February, died in 1752 according to the old calendar and in 1753 according to the new one. That is why you may find 1752/3 on a tombstone. If you had been born in January 1752 and lived long enough to see January 1851, you would have celebrated your 100th (*not* your 99th) birthday. That is why they took to inscribing 'OS' meaning Old Style and NS meaning New Style.

Also in, or near, the churchyard we may be lucky enough to find an old stone cross which pre-dates the building of the church. This marked the spot where the early missionaries held their services.

We may even find some stocks where wrongdoers were sentenced to sit and undergo their humiliating, but effective punishment. Try to imagine what it must have been like to sit for many hours – or days – unable to move your legs and unable to rest your back. Worst of all, what happens when you need to go to the loo!

*Burford church, with its tall graceful spire, is one of the largest churches in Oxfordshire. Note the splendid 18th-century tombs.*

*13th-century broach spire with wooden shingles,*
*Shere, Surrey.*

Now to the church itself. There may be Saxon stonework at the base of the tower, which is usually at the west end. The earliest towers had low squat roofs which, over the years, developed into the tall graceful spires of the 14th century.

My grandfather particularly loved the *broach* spires of the 13th century, where an octagonal spire is made to slightly overlap the square tower on which it sits. These were often covered with tiles made of oak or elm – *shingles*.

*A view of the superb broach spire at Horsham, West Sussex;
see also Frontispiece.*

*The unusual belfry at Brooklands in Kent.*

He had wonderful stories to tell of the spire-like belfry which stands beside the church at Brooklands in Kent. Sometimes he would maintain that the builders had completed the church and had quite forgotten the belfry; at other times, he said that it had blown off in a gale. The truth is more likely to be that the foundations in the Kent marsh were not strong enough to take the extra weight.(Although local legend has it that it fell off in surprise when a virgin came to be married in the church.)

Let us look at the walls of the church. Mostly they were built of local materials (stone, brick or flint) and strengthened by buttresses. Norman walls were so thick they hardly needed buttresses at all, but as the centuries passed and knowledge and experience of stresses and strains improved, the walls became thinner and the buttresses became finer, more pronounced and a decorative feature of the exterior. The same sort of progress can be seen if you look at modern engineering feats such as the suspension bridges over the Severn or the Humber and see how far techniques have advanced since the construction of the solid medieval bridges with their short spans which so delighted my grandfather.

Above: *King John's Bridge which spans the River Avon at
Tewkesbury, Gloucestershire. Close to the bridge stands
the Black Bear, the oldest inn in Tewkesbury, a half-timbered
building that is supposed to date from 1308.*

Above right: *Trotton Bridge in Sussex.*

Below right: *Eashing Bridge in Surrey.*

*Three typical medieval bridges
with their solid stonework and short spans.*

TROTTON BRIDGE
SUSSEX 1913.
E.E.F.

Before gutters were provided, the only way of preventing rainwater from running down church walls was to allow the roof to project considerably over the walls. This projection had to be supported by a series of brackets known as *corbels*, and these were often carved as grotesque faces. When gutters came in the collected rainwater was thrown out and away from the walls through spouts called *gargoyles* (from the Old French word *gargouille* meaning 'throat' – hence gargle), which were often carved in the shapes of devils or dragons. Later on in the 14th and 15th centuries, the guttering was hidden behind parapet walls which were castellated for decorative effect.

*A spire with its roof projecting over the walls of the church tower supported by corbels.*

*For the keen ecclesiologist, a blocked-up doorway*
*poses many questions.*

You will often see the outline of a door or window long since filled in. Why? Each individual example may provide a different answer – if it is known. The north side of the church may be Early English, the south side Decorated and the whole of the chancel Perpendicular. (As I said, it is a detective story – how, why and when was this church altered?) A Norman doorway may be protected and hidden by a porch from a later period. In medieval times, many important functions took place in the porch. Here women knelt to be 'churched' after the birth of a child. Here was where the beginning of the service of baptism took place. Here the marriage banns were called and part of the marriage service took place. Much civil business was transacted here, and it was also a convenient place to exhibit public notices.

*A magnificent Norman doorway is covered by a porch
from a later period.*

*Porches vary enormously in size and design.*

*Porches played an important role in medieval times.*

Sometimes a room – called a *parvise* – was built above the porch where the priest could sleep and also teach the local children in what was the earliest type of school. Although porches may be found on the north side of a church, they are usually on the south – and, just to confuse you, sometimes on both sides.

Did you know that the police are not allowed to enter a church unless invited? Inside the building the church wardens are responsible for good behaviour. And ever since the murder of Thomas à Becket at Canterbury in 1170, no one is allowed to carry a drawn sword in a church; if a serving officer in the armed forces is married in uniform, he must leave his sheathed sword behind before he enters the chancel.

On the outer walls of the church, we can often see a cross carved into the stonework. Originally there were twelve on the outer and twelve on the inner walls. They are 'consecration crosses' and were anointed by the bishop during the ceremony of consecration which took place after the building was finished and before Mass could be said for the first time.

Somewhere near the south door, we may see a sundial on the wall – or even a primitive Mass sundial with just a small hole with several lines radiating from it, scratched into the stone. A traveller could place a stock in the hole and, provided the sun was shining, the shadow would give him an idea of how long it would be before the next Mass was to be said.

Let us hope that this church we are visiting has a splendid old door. In early times, they were constructed of a double thickness of oak planks, vertical outside and horizontal inside, fixed together with stout wrought-iron nails; the hinges, locks and handles were also made of the same wrought iron. As time went by, the results of the blacksmith's craft became more decorative, until the 14th century, when for some reason the joiner ousted the blacksmith and the doors became the surface for mouldings and carvings in wood. Before we pass through, just look up; there may be some beautiful stone carving on the *tympanum* – the space over the door and below the surrounding arch.

*Imposing porch with a room above, possibly for the priest. Note the sundial.*

*The church at Cowden in Kent, with its broach spire
and small room above the porch.*

*Broken stoup just inside the door of Dunsfold church in Surrey.*

Just inside the door, we may see a *stoup* which was broken by the anti-papist wreckers sent out by Henry VIII. This contained holy water into which the faithful could dip a finger and make the sign of the cross on themselves.

Look next at the columns. I always want to hug the great fat Norman ones – they have stood there patiently bearing a vast load on their heads for 900 years.

*Massive Norman columns and vaulting with zig-zag*
*decoration, Round church, Cambridge.*

Give them a hug – they love it. All you can do with Early English columns is marvel: can those slender shafts really carry any weight? You would soon know if you took one away. They remind me of a very severe Victorian aunt, carrying a tightly rolled umbrella and wearing a hat of waxed flowers. The Decorated ones look like knights in armour crowned with flowers, about to joust for a lady's hand. The Perpendicular column is cool – very cool and anorexic.

*A slender Perpendicular column looking very cool
and anorexic.*

If we are very lucky this church may contain the remains of some wall paintings which will help us to appreciate what the inside of a medieval church must have looked like. Just imagine the walls covered with such paintings and with their colours undimmed. Apart from their decorative effect, they illustrated the Christian story to a largely illiterate congregation. Incidents from the lives of Christ and the Saints filled the walls and, almost invariably, over the chancel arch was a large painting of the Day of Judgement – the 'Doom' as it was called – with open graves at the bottom, on the left the Good ascending to Heaven to be received by Christ and, on the right, the Bad descending to Hell to be tortured by devils.

All of these wonderful paintings were obliterated with whitewash by the iconoclasts of Edward VI or Cromwell, and their damaged remains have only quite recently been rediscovered.

Somewhere at the west end will be the font. Whole books have been written on fonts, and they fascinated by grandfather. In the early days of conversion, it was the practice for the adults to stand in the font and have the holy water poured over them; the font was therefore a stone tub placed on the floor. In later years, where those to be baptised were mostly babies of the faithful, they were totally immersed, so for convenience, the tubs were raised on a low plinth. Later still, when all that was required was for the infant to have the holy water poured on its head, the fonts became much smaller and were raised even higher.

From the 13th century, all fonts had covers which were locked to prevent the theft of the holy water for dubious purposes.

*Jacobean font with a decorated font cover at*
*Chiddingstone, Kent.*

*A highly ornate font cover with its pulley and bracket*
*at Knaresborough, North Yorkshire.*

We can frequently see the iron staples – or the holes where they had been fixed – which once formed part of the fastening. In later periods, these font covers became more and more decorated, sometimes needing pulleys to lift them. Fonts have an infinite variety of shapes: simple stone tubs like the kitchen coppers our grandparents had:

others superbly moulded in lead:

enormous square ones, sometimes in marble from Tournai in France:

some intricately carved:

some with signs of the Zodiac:

some resembling capitals of fallen pillars:

At the end of one of the aisles is a chapel with its own altar, possibly fenced off with a wrought-iron screen – a *parclose*. This is either a guild chapel or a mortuary chapel in which would lie the remains of the local lord of the manor. In medieval times, the various guilds were very powerful and were virtually closed shops. Blacksmiths, carpenters, masons, wheelwrights and other craftsmen could not work unless they belonged to, and had served an apprenticeship with, a particular guild, and they were sworn to secrecy not to divulge details of their craft. These guilds became very wealthy, and to echo their status, they erected superb chapels in certain churches.

*A simple stone font sits in the foreground, with a hagioscope cut into the wall to the right of the arch.*

*Simple oak benches situated in front of a Saxon arch.*

That hole cut through the thickness of the chancel wall is called a *squint*, or, better still, a *hagioscope*, and allowed worshippers in a chapel to see the priest elevate the host at the main altar. Alternatively, if two priests were to say Mass at the same time, the second one in the chapel could watch the first so that they would elevate the host together.

During the Middle Ages, there were no pews in the churches, and the congregation – when not kneeling – stood throughout the service. However, continuous stone benches were provided along the side walls for the sick and infirm. This practice gave rise to the expression 'the weakest to the wall'. Sometimes we may find a squint (or hagioscope) cut through in such a position so that the weak could see the altar.

Pews as we see them today began to be installed in the 14th century. The earliest were simple oak benches, but as we have already seen, the wood carvers

*Carved square-headed pew ends in the West Country,*
*probably Bere Regis in Dorset.*

exercised their craft on the bench ends until, by the 15th century, they had
produced some of their finest work on the side panels and the tops of the
bench ends, which they formed into what are known as 'poppyheads'. These
have always reminded me of the three Prince of Wales feathers, with the two
outer ones drooping.

*15th-century bench ends carved into 'poppyheads' at*
*Shoreham-by-Sea, West Sussex.*

*Box pews with doors kept out drafts at Shere in
Surrey.*

A later invention was the box pew which, once the door was closed, added
greatly to the comfort of the occupants in the draughty unheated church.
Many of these were for the private use of local families.

The lords of the manor, or squires, went one better and built their own family pews with fireplaces and curtains and furnished with tables and armchairs.

Now we come to the chancel arch which leads to the chancel – the holiest part of the church – and therefore the arch is usually an object of some splendour. So good was this, in fact, that when rebuilding other parts of the church, later masons would often treat with awe and respect the superb workmanship of their predecessors and leave well alone. Sometimes the only evidence of Norman work in an otherwise much later building is the chancel arch deeply cut in the famous zig-zag, or chevron, pattern.

*Norman arch with zig-zag decoration, leading to the chancel at Mottisfont, Hampshire.*

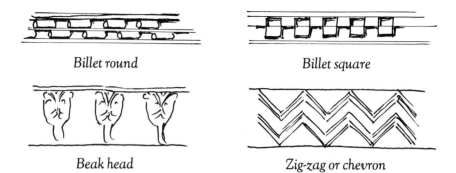

*Billet round*　　　　　　　　　　*Billet square*

*Beak head*　　　　　　　　　*Zig-zag or chevron*

Some people will tell you that the simple Norman artisans cut this pattern with an axe. A load of rubbish. No sculptor worth his pay, especially a man who the next minute could carve out a beak-head or billet moulding, would use an axe.

Before the Reformation, all churches had a *rood screen*. Let me explain: Across the chancel arch and dividing the chancel from the nave was a screen either of stone or wood with a central doorway to allow access. The top of the screen was level with the top of the columns at the point where the arch itself began. On this stood the Rood – a figure of Christ on the Cross with the Virgin Mary and St John (the beloved disciple) kneeling on either side. (The word 'rood' is of ancient origin; its original meaning was 'wood' and was applied to the Cross; we still find the word used – e.g. Holy*rood* Palace and in the word 'rod'.) It was necessary to gain access to the Rood so that candles could be lit and, during Lent, the crucifix could be covered with a rood cloth.

*Rood staircase providing access to the Rood above the chancel arch.*

Therefore, the top of the screen had to be wide enough for people to walk about on it, and a small spiral staircase was formed in the wall to provide access. During the Commonwealth in the 17th century, these Roods were deemed to be 'popish' and the order went out that they – together with other Roman Catholic emblems – should be destroyed. While many rood screens still exist, a number were also removed, and what we are left with is a staircase, or the remains of one, leading to a doorway high up on the chancel arch and opening on to nothing. They are usually to be found on the left hand (north) side of the church, and quite often give the appearance of having been cut into the wall after the arch was built.

*Rood screen and stairs leading to the rood loft, with*
*a small hagioscope cut into the wall, Lydford, Devon.*

Beside the chancel arch, we will find the pulpit and the lectern – sometimes combined at a later period into the form of a two- or three-decker: the lowest was where the clerk sat, in the middle was a lectern for the reader, and the highest 'deck' was the pulpit for the sermon. As with fonts, there is enormous variety in the design of pulpits. At Didling in West Sussex, the pulpit has been

*A Perpendicular style chancel screen and pulpit.*

Above: *A wooden pulpit, probably Jacobean.*

Below: *Pulpit with a tester to reflect the preacher's voice.*

*A fine pulpit and lectern at Worth, Sussex.*

made up of the remains of an old chest. The usual brass lectern, on which the Bible rests on the outstretched wings of an eagle, originated in the 16th century, but earlier wooden ones can be found.

Now turn and look up at the roof: it may be vaulted in stone. Imagine the inside of an umbrella with the spokes carrying a thin web between them. The stone ribs are the strength of the vault, the panels between are, as it were, the ceiling between the joists. If each bay has four panels between the spokes, this is known as a *quadripartite* vault:

*Detail of superb 15th-century timber roof construction.*

If it has six, it is known as a *sexpartite* vault. If there are many extra ribs (called *liernes*) running between the main ribs, it is known as a *lierne* vault. Sometimes these are arranged in the shaped of stars: it then is called a *stellar* vault.

Actually stone vaults are rather uncommon in parish churches – we are far more likely to find that the underside of the roof is made of timber, and of complex construction. Go up into your own loft and you may begin to understand the problems faced by the early carpenters. Your loft will be hidden away in the roof space, but medieval craftsmen expected their work to be seen and, at the same time, to be strong enough to carry an immensely heavy roof over a single large space, supported only by the outer walls. Without diagrams, it is difficult to explain the solutions to the problem: the simplest was to use a series of tie-beams across the width of the building, each of which would have consisted of a complete tree – some 30 odd feet long and 12 inches square. On these could be mounted, in the middle, a vertical *kingpost*, jointed to collar beams and braces to hold up the rafters. The disadvantage of this system was that the tie beams cut horizontally right across the church interior and effectively reduced the height.

*The only one of my grandfather's drawings showing
a kingpost. Note the massive tie-beams.*

*A barrel roof in the chancel.*

One alternative was produced by a series of braces with flattened surfaces, which were then boarded over to give the effect of being inside a barrel – hence its name, *barrel roof*. In an effort to decrease the span, another idea evolved. Projecting brackets resting on corbels were placed along the wall, and the braces – similar to those in the barrel roof – were mounted on them. The brackets are known as *hammer beams*. It was only a short step for the carpenters to construct a second series of brackets on top of the first, thus producing one of the glories of the 15th century: the *double hammer-beam roof*.

As the chancel is the holiest part of the church, the roof there is usually much more complex or more beautifully decorated than the rest. Let us now reverently approach this special place. Up a step and through the chancel arch.

On either side will be the choir stalls – some still lit by candles. Many will be quite plain and functional, but others may be beautifully carved with poppyhead ornaments and fretted hoods. Look now for the *misericords*: you may find something which will give you great delight and which, alone, will make your whole visit worthwhile. Misericords are tip-up seats with a sort of bracket on the underside fixed in such a way that when, during the service, the chorister was required to stand for some considerable time, he could actually be half-sitting on the ledge of the upturned seat and still give the impression that he was standing. These frequently beautifully carved brackets often depict most irreligious subjects – as might befit the part of the anatomy that rested on them! The wood carvers could really let themselves go and, unhindered, choose any subject that appealed to their fertile imaginations. I will not spoil your fun by telling you of my own discoveries, but please be very careful in the way you handle the seats – don't bang them about. They have been there for many hundreds of years, and with careful treatment, they will continue to give solace to some and pleasure to others.

Here in the chancel, the lords of the manor or other wealthy parishioners were buried – the nearer to the altar, the more important the person. The tombs are often of superb craftsmanship. Some are of the table type, and some of these have effigies of the deceased reclining on them. Knights depicted in armour often have their heads resting on their helmets and their feet on small lions. The ladies often have their feet on small dogs to symbolize fidelity –

*A misericord with a carved head of 'The Green Man'*
*supporting the bracket.*

*A magnificently ornate 15th-century tomb*
*in the chancel.*

*Sir Alexander Culpeper and his wife lie side by side in effigy*
*at Goudhurst, Kent.*

*Lord Oxenbridge is depicted in full armour with*
*his feet resting on a fierce lion.*

*An impressive table tomb in a central position
and as close to the altar as possible.*

however, the absence of a dog does not necessarily symbolize infidelity! Around the sides of some tombs, we may see little figures known as *weepers*. If not angels or saints, they will represent the children of the deceased, boys on one side, girls on the other. If one of them is carrying a skull, this means that that child died before the deceased. Here, and possibly in the nave, we may see some *brasses* – thin sheets of metal let into the stone and then engraved with a likeness of the deceased. From these effigies, we can learn an enormous amount about the costumes of the period. However, over the years, many have been destroyed or stolen, leaving only the indentation in the stone.

On the left-hand (north) wall, there may be an *Easter sepulchre* – a recess cut into the wall and often surrounded by stone carving. In there on Good Friday were placed the host (the consecrated Communion bread) and the altar crucifix, which were guarded until they were removed with much ceremony on Easter morning and placed on the high altar, symbolizing the burial and resurrection of Christ. More often you will find another somewhat smaller recess called an *aumbry*. Originally, this was enclosed by a wooden door – you will see the holes of the hinges and locks – and here were kept the vessels containing the holy oils used for baptism, confirmation and the last rites.

*A family tomb with indistinct 'weepers'*
*around the base.*

On the right-hand (south) wall, near the altar, will be another recess which, on closer examination, will prove to hold a basin with a little drain hole. Here the vessels used in the Mass could be washed, and the water, which might well contain remnants of the consecrated wine and wafers, could drain out through the wall on to the equally holy ground of the churchyard. This recess and its basin is called a *piscina* – from the Latin word for fish, *piscis*.

*A piscina cut into the wall of the chancel*
*close to the altar, Wonersh, Surrey.*

Also on the south side, you will often find glorious things called *sedilia*, another Latin word meaning 'seats'. (Don't be put off – you will pick up all these words in time, and soon will be surprised to find that your friends have never heard of sedilia.) Although occasionally there may be two or four seats, sedilia usually comprise three seats built into the wall and topped with elaborately carved canopies.

The seat nearest the altar – and usually the most impressive – was reserved for the priest and the other two for the deacons. Here they could rest during the long services.

Now we come to the high altar on the east wall. In Old Testament times, altars were originally flat stones on which sacrifices were made. Then the early Christians used the tombs of martyrs in the Catacombs of Rome as altars on which to celebrate Mass. Later they were made of wood until Lanfranc, Archbishop of Canterbury in the 11th century, decreed that all altars were to be made of stone; they are usually incised on the top with five crosses,

*A three-seated sedilia combined with a piscina*
*with a shelf above for holding the holy vessels.*

*Another magnificent example of a piscina and sedilia at Dunsfold, Surrey.*

symbolizing the five wounds of Christ. The altar is covered with cloths of different colours: green for ordinary days, white for the chief feasts, red for martyrs and violet for fasts. Some altars are of delightful simplicity while others have a splendiferous reredos rising up behind them and often covering the lower part of the best window in the church. The ceiling above is also often highly decorated. Very few stone altars are to be found as most were destroyed at the time of the Reformation because they usually contained the bones of popish saints.

In the Middle Ages, the clergy received tithes from their parishioners and were often paid 'in kind'. As result, in certain churches a 'pen' was constructed to hold the various animals that the priest received. (Just imagine the noise during a service!) Dogs also roamed freely and – horror upon horror – were sometimes guilty of lifting a leg against the altar. In the early 17th century, Archbishop Laud was so appalled at this that he ordered rails to be erected in all churches to protect the altar.

*Details of different altar rails. The one below is Jacobean.*

*Here the altar rails separate the apsidal*
*chancel from the base of the central tower.*

*A redundant doorway.*

The congregation could also kneel at this rail to receive Communion. Some churches employed a man to keep children and dogs in order, and provided him with expanding scissor-like tongs to grasp an offending dog by the neck and eject it.

Also in the chancel is either a small door or the blocked up remains of one. This allowed the priest private access to his own part of the church.

Let us now retrace our steps.

Around the walls we can see many *mural tablets* recording the deaths and recalling the lives of local dignitaries. Before you know where you are, you will be piecing together the genealogy of these families. Some of the early inscriptions are in charming but excruciatingly bad verse, so always carry a notebook with you; otherwise you are bound to have forgotten them by the

*In Memoriam.*

time you get home. The same applies to the inscriptions you have seen in the churchyard.

I know I should be a devotee of stained glass but I am not. You will throw up your hands in horror, but I am unrepentant. I can touch, feel and thrill to stonework and carving, but stained glass, no. To look out through a medieval window glazed with clear glass and see a real tree gently waving in the breeze lifts my heart, and I rejoice at the conjuncture of the God-made and the man-made. But not through stained glass. Sorry about this, but I am what I am – colour-blind.

Oh, look – up there – high up on the western wall is the little window into the priest's room in the tower.

Most churches also possess individual things of historical interest. I am thinking particularly of one that has an original pitchpipe on which the choirmaster would blow to give the correct pitch to his choristers. Another has a Roman altar stone at the base of the tower. Another has the cradle in which the Dean Swift slept as a baby. Others have pieces of armour hung above the tombs of the original owners. You will enjoy making your own discoveries as I have.

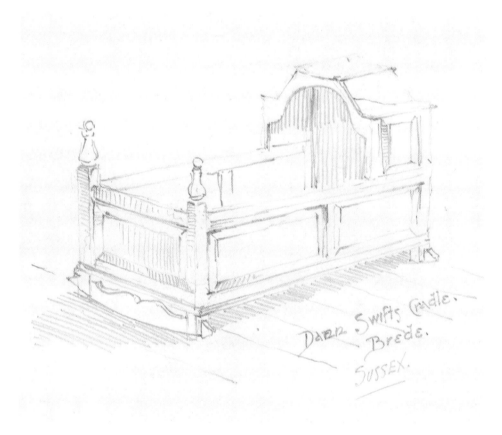

*Disgracefully, this cradle was stolen from the
church some ten years ago.*

PETWORTH CHURCH.
1910

*His jousting days are over, and the warrior's*
*helmet rusts away above his tomb.*

*No longer does this chest contain valuables.*
*Below is another of my grandfather's favourite bridges.*

*But for its spire, this could easily be a medieval castle.*

Against a wall, we may see a massive chest with great iron hinges and straps. It could well date from the 12th century. The early chests were hewn from solid tree trunks. Some chests were fitted with three locks: one could be opened by the priest and the other two by the church wardens. In them were kept not only the valuable church plate and vestments but all the parish records and accounts. The presence of these chests and their contents reminds us that the church was the centre, not only of the religious, but also the social life of the parishioners. Life began and ended – from baptism to burial – in the church. All communal activities took place here, including festivals of all kinds and even the village dance, so it was natural that the church became the repository of anything that belonged collectively to the villagers. Fire fighting equipment was stored here as well as musical instruments for the village orchestra, who played in this, the only public building. Bread was kept in the *dole cupboard* for distribution to the poor after the Sunday service. I believe that, until very recently, it was an offence for any public clock to show the wrong time: this law was left over from the days when the church clock was probably the only timepiece in the locality and everyone depended on its accuracy. In a rural community, it was also necessary to know the direction of the wind, so on the top of every church tower or spire could be seen a weather vane.

Ewell.

19 Sep.ˢ 1896

*A ruined tower rises romantically above the
mushrooming gravestones, Ewell, Surrey.*

*An interesting combination of roof lines
emerge from a massive tower, Fetcham, Surrey.*

By the particular sounds of individual bells ringing out from the belfry, villagers could deduce all that was happening in their parish. It is still true of most villages that the church is the most durable building of architectural merit, and I harbour an ecumenical dream that they will return to being used for multifarious purposes.

Endeavouring to remove all secular activities from churches, the Victorians caused countless village and church halls to be built. Every parish had to have one, and they were and are used for many things. The dramatic society performs there, whist drives are held, youth clubs meet, public meetings are held, the Women's Institute meets, exhibitions take place, flower shows and the like are displayed, while the church itself is used by only a handful of people and only for a few hours a week.

I would like all these activities to return to the place where they belong – the nave of the church. Sell off the church halls, use the money to provide double-glazing, control the draughts, install good heating equipment (perhaps underfloor heating, as has been done in Chichester Cathedral) and cooking facilities. Let us have dancing in the nave (and not only in the aisles), plays

*Weather vanes revolve above three very different*
*roofs. At Ashurst, Kent, a free-standing sundial*
*on the right supplements another above the porch door*
*— was one for summer-time?*

WINCHELSEA CHURCH.

A.F.Fuller.

*Little remains of the once enormous church of*
*St Thomas the Apostle, Winchelsea, East Sussex.*

*Windows of three different styles, a clock, a*
*broach spire with a fine weathercock – let us go in!*

(secular as well as spiritual) performed there, village fêtes held inside as well as outside and stalls erected for the sale of cakes, jam and white elephants. I know that most ecclesiastics who may be reading this will be horrified, but our churches – and by that I mean the buildings themselves – must live again as the centres of their communities and not be allowed to crumble into dusty museums only of interest to dusty ecclesiologists. Of course, the sanctity of the chancel must not be violated, but the nave – historically the province of the people – is the perfectly logical place for such activities. And why should schools be closed to allow polling booths to be put up for local and national elections? These too should take place in the church.

There is, of course, the problem of the pews. Very few churches have pews of historic or artistic merit, even though some blinkered ecclesiologists would have us believe that they exist in every church. While some must be preserved *in situ*, the others could be altered, if necessary, to provide movable seating or (and I can hear you shudder) sold, but certainly not destroyed. And, while I am on my high horse, may I suggest that all religious denominations should use the same building – albeit at different times. Chancels can be curtained off and portable tables and pulpits trundled in for the Nonconformists. Statues, incense and stoups can be returned to cupboards after a Roman Catholic service. A crucifix can easily be replaced by a cross and, who knows, we may soon find that we are all Christians one way or the other and love our neighbours as ourselves.

*Such a delightful object
makes giving a pleasure.*

On that hopeful, but contentious note, I think we had better be moving off. But before we do, over there is an ancient offertory box. You will notice that it is constructed of oak, bound about with iron straps and secured with locks. At the church of St Agnes at Cawston in Norfolk, there is a fine example, hewn out of a single piece of oak. Under the iron lid, which is secured by two primitive combination locks, is an inverted iron cup which prevents anyone trying to retrieve the coins. (Obviously some of our forebears were as untrustworthy as some of us are today.) That box is no longer in use, but a modern variation will be found near the main door. Please put in all you can afford. This building and many others, which house the beautiful work of so many anonymous craftsmen, cannot continue to exist without our help.

I don't think my grandfather would agree with some of the things I have said, but I remain eternally grateful to him for introducing me to an abiding interest.

# Glossary

*Abacus* the flat slab on the top of a *capital* which supports the superstructure

*Apse* In plan, a semi-circular end to the *chancel* (usually east end)

*Aumbry* a cupboard, recessed into the north wall of the *chancel*, to hold sacred vessels

*Ballflower Moulding* a series of carved balls incised with what looks like a three-leafed clover

*Barrel Vault* semi-circular ceiling, sometimes called a tunnel vault

*Beakhead Moulding* pattern of little faces with pointed beaks

*Billet Moulding* short rectangular or semi-circular blocks placed at regular intervals in a hollow

*Blind Arcade* a series of arches, sometimes interlaced, used to decorate the flat surface of a wall

*Boss* projection of wood or stone at the intersection of a *vault's* ribs, usually carved

*Broach Spire* an octagonal spire sitting on, and overlapping, a square tower

*Canopy* the ornamental head over a niche or stained-glass figure

*Capital* the topmost part of a pier or column that supports everything above it

*Cartouche* an elaborate wall tablet with inscribed writing in an ornamental frame

*Chamfer* a bevelled edge

*Chancel* the part of the church that contains the altar – the province of the clergy

*Chantry Chapel* a chapel within a church wherein Masses could be said for the founder

*Chevron Moulding* zig-zag moulding

*Clerestory* the topmost level of the wall, pierced with windows, below the roof and above the *triforium*

*Corbel* a sort of bracket, often decorated, projecting from a wall to carry a weight

*Crocket* a purely ornamental thing, looking like a curled leaf or a pig's tail, projecting from an otherwise plain edge

*Cusp* a pointed decorative feature incorporated into Gothic tracery

*Dripstone* a projecting moulding over a door or window to keep the rain off

*Easter Sepulchre* a recess, usually in the north wall of the *chancel*, with a decorative *canopy* and often above a tomb

*Ecclesiologists* enthusiasts who devote themselves to the study of churches and their architecture

*Entablature* the horizontal sections above the columns (in classical architecture – *metope*, *triglyph*, architrave and so on)

*Fan Vault* a vault comprising a convex, fan-like projection of ribs

*Finial* the bit at the very top of a spire, pinnacle or gable

*Gargoyle* a waterspout projecting

from the top of a wall, often decorated with heads, animals or grotesques

*Geometric Tracery* tracery made up of simple circles, *trefoils, quatrefoils,* and so on

*Hagioscope* see *Squint*

*Hammerbeam Roof* a wooden roof built up from brackets projecting from the wall

*Kingpost* the central vertical member of a roof truss

*Label Stops* the ends of a moulding that frames an arch, often decorated with carved heads

*Lancet* a narrow pointed window in Early English architecture, often grouped in threes, fives or sevens

*Lierne Vault* vaulting largely comprising small ribs between the main members

*Lych-gate* the covered gate to the churchyard

*Metope* the blocks between the fluted *triglyphs* that make up the frieze in classical *entablature*

*Misericords* a hinged seat, the underside of which is often elaborately carved

*Moulding* a continuous line with a decorative profile

*Mullion* a vertical bar that divides a window, usually made of stone

*Mural Tablets* a stone affixed to a wall, with inscribed writing

*Nave* the main body of the church, normally to the west of the *chancel*

*Ogee* an arch or *moulding* with a double-curve profile like the figure S

*Parclose* a decorative screen dividing a chapel from the main part of the church

*Parvise* a word often incorrectly used to describe a room over a porch

*Piscina* a small, stone washbasin on the south side of the altar

*Plate Tracery* the earliest form of

*tracery,* produced by placing two *lancet* windows side by side under a pointed arch and cutting through the stonework between the tops of the two windows

*Quadripartite Vault* a vault above a bay, divided by ribs into four parts

*Quatrefoil* a rounded, moulded opening in four sections – like a four-leafed clover

*Quoins* dressed corner stones

*Reredos* a screen behind and above the altar

*Rood* a Crucifix

*Rood Screen* a screen between the *chancel* and *nave* carrying the *Rood,* together with statues of the Virgin Mary and St John

*Scalloped Capital* a Norman *capital* with radiating ridges and grooves

*Sedilia* seats for the priests on the south side of the *chancel*

*Sexpartite Vault* a vault above a bay, divided by ribs into six parts

*Shaft* the part of a column between the base and the *capital*

*Shingles* roofing tiles made of wood

*Squinch* small arches across the corners of a square tower to produce the seating for an octagonal spire

*Squint (Hagioscope)* a small opening cut through a wall to effect a view of the altar

*Swag* a decorative motif of flowers, fruit or foliage suspended between two points

*Tester* a canopy above a pulpit

*Tracery* the ornamental stonework within upper parts of windows

*Transept* the parts of a church to the north or south of the crossing

*Transom* a horizontal bar that divides a window, usually made of stone

*Trefoil* a rounded, moulded opening in three sections – like a three-leafed clover

*Triforium* the space above the arcade but below the *clerestory*

*Triglyph* the fluted blocks that alternate with *metopes*

*Tympanum* the space above the door lintel and within the door arch

*Vault* a roof or covering in stone or brick

*Volute Capital* a capital with spiral/scroll ornament

*Voussoirs* the wedge-shaped stones that form an arch

*Weepers* small figures carved around the base of tombs

# Further Reading

A few of the books mentioned in this list are out of print but it is hoped that the interested reader may be able to track down some of them.

*Buildings of England series, The*, by Sir Nikolaus Pevsner, and others, Penguin

Betjeman, Sir John (ed). *Collins Guide to Parish Churches of England and Wales, including the Isle of Man.* Collins, revised edn, 1980

Bond, Francis. *Fonts and Font Covers* (1908). Waterstone, revised edn, 1985

Bond, Francis. *Screens and Galleries in English Churches.* Oxford University Press, 1908

Bond, Francis. *Wood Carvings in English Churches* (2 vols). Oxford University Press, 1910

Caiger-Smith, A. *English Mediaeval Mural Paintings.* Oxford University Press, 1963

Clifton-Taylor, Alec. *English Parish Churches as Works of Art.* Batsford, 2nd edn, 1986

Cook, G.H. *The English Mediaeval Parish Church.* Phoenix House, 1955

Cox, J. Charles. *Pulpits, Lecterns and Organs in English Churches.* Oxford University Press, 1915

Cox, J. Charles and Charles B. Ford. *The Parish Churches of England.* Batsford, 1941

Cox, J. Charles and Alfred Harvey. *English Church Furniture* (1907). EP Publishing, facsimile edn, 1973

Crewe, Sarah. *Stained Glass in England, c. 1180-c. 1540.* HMSO, for Royal Commission on Historical Monuments of England, 1987

Crossley, F.H. *English Church Monuments, A.D. 1150-1550: an introduction to the story of tombs and effigies of the mediaeval period.* Batsford, 1921.

Dirsztay, Patricia. *Church Furnishings* (A NADFAS Guide). Routlege & Kegan Paul, 1978

Dixon, Roger and Stefan Muthesius. *Victorian Architecture.* Thames & Hudson, 1978

Farmer, David Hugh (ed). *The Oxford*

*Dictionary of Saints.* Oxford University Press, 1979

Fletcher, Banister. *A History of Architecture on the Comparative Method.* Athlone Press, 17th edn, 1967

Harris, John and Jill Lever. *Illustrated Glossary of Architecture.* Faber, 1966

Harrison, Martin. *Victorian Stained Glass.* Barrie & Jenkins, 1980

Hutton, Graham. *English Parish Churches;* introductory notes by Graham Hutton, notes on the plates by Olive Cook, photographs by Edwin Smith. Thames & Hudson, 1976

Jones, Lawrence E. *The Observer's Book of Old English Churches.* Frederick Warne, 1965

Jones, Lawrence E. *The Beauty of English Churches.* Constable, 1978

Kemp, Brian. *English Church Monuments.* Batsford, 1980

Needham, A. *How to Study an Old Church.* Batsford, 1957

Page-Phillips, John. *Macklins's Monumental Brasses.* Allen & Unwin, 1968

Penny, Nicholas. *Church Monuments in Romantic England.* Yale University Press, 1977

Randall, Gerald. *Church Furnishing and Decoration in England and Wales.* Batsford, 1980

Rodwell, Warwick and James Bentley. *Our Christian Heritage.* George Philip, 1984

Shipley, Revd Orby. *A Glossary of Ecclesiastical Terms.* Rivingtons, 1872

Stratton, Arthur. *The Styles of English Architecture.* Batsford

Stratton, Arthur. *The Orders of Architecture.* Batsford, 1931

Thomson, Barbara and Wendy Trewin. *Embroidered Church Kneelers.* Batsford, 1987

Whiffen, Marcus. *Stuart and Georgian Churches: the architecture of the Church of England outside London, 1603-1837.* Batsford, 1948

Woodforde, Christopher. *English Stained and Painted Glass.* Oxford University Press, 1954.

# Index

Page numbers in *italic* refer to the illustrations

# INDEX